THE
SLIMMING
AIR FRYER
COOKBOOK

**The Best Recipes for Cutting the Fat and Keeping the
Flavour in your Favourite Fried Foods**

Ella Sanders

ROBINSON

ROBINSON

First published in the US in 2022 by St Martin's Press as *The Skinny Air Fryer Cookbook*

First published in Great Britain in 2023 by Robinson

1 3 5 7 9 10 8 6 4 2

Design by Joanna Williams
Production by Laura White
Photography under license from Shutterstock.com
except photo on page 39 by Allan Penn

A CIP catalogue record for this book
is available from the British Library.

ISBN: 978-1-47214-857-5

Printed and bound in Great Britain by Bell and Bain Ltd, Glasgow

Papers used by Robinson are from well-managed forests
and other responsible sources.

Robinson
An imprint of
Little, Brown Book Group
Carmelite House
50 Victoria Embankment
London EC4Y 0DZ

An Hachette UK Company
www.hachette.co.uk

www.littlebrown.co.uk

How To Books are published by Robinson, an imprint of Little, Brown Book Group.
We welcome proposals from authors who have first-hand experience of their subjects.
Please set out the aims of your book, its target market and its suggested contents
in an email to howto@littlebrown.co.uk

contents

getting started

Whether you want to drop 5 pounds or 3 stone, focusing on what you eat is the best way to lose weight safely and effectively. In fact, research suggests that cooking at home may be the easiest strategy for realizing the benefits of enjoying healthier meals. You can better control which ingredients you use as well as portion sizes. But what about cooking methods? Does that mean you'll have to subsist on a lifetime of smoothies and steamed vegetables? Not if you have an air fryer!

Your air fryer is hands down the most useful kitchen appliance to help you reach your weight loss goals, because it can help you enjoy familiar flavours without the added fats that come with cooking methods like traditional frying. This cookbook is filled with more than 75 delicious recipes designed to satisfy without weighing you down. You'll love slimming dishes like Chicken Parmigiana (page 62), Spicy Sicilian Chicken Drumsticks (page 102), Crab Cakes with Roasted Corn-Pepper Relish (page 114), Ham and Cheese Calzones (page 73), and Guilt-Free Veggie Spring Rolls (page 38). And you can enjoy sweet but smart indulgences with lighter

desserts like Glazed Doughnuts (page 119), Peanut Butter Chocolate Chip Cookies (page 125), and Chocolate Lava Cake for Two (page 126). Your air fryer makes it easy to get big flavour with slimming results—it's your secret weapon for weight loss!

benefits of your air fryer

If weight loss is your goal, an air fryer can be such a valuable asset in the kitchen. The benefits you get with an air fryer that can also make losing weight easier include:

Less fat. Air fryers circulate hot air to cook foods, resulting in the same crisp exterior and tender interior produced by conventional deep fryers but with far less fat. Beyond frying, the air fryer can also roast, steam, grill, and bake. Whatever cooking method you turn to the air fryer for, it improves the process with faster, more even heat—and delicious results.

Speedy cooking. Not only do air fryers tend to speed the cooking time for most recipes (the circulation of hot air means foods cook faster), but you'll also find that using an air fryer usually involves less hassle than traditional cooking methods. So you'll stick with all of the super-easy recipes in this book. Need to check for doneness? Just slide open the basket to take a quick look. Need to turn the food to ensure even baking? Give the basket a quick shake. That said, models vary, so use the cooking times in this collection as a guide versus a rule and adjust accordingly.

Less mess. Air frying is considerably less messy than deep-fat frying. The units are self-contained, so you don't need to contend with splatters. And because most air fryer baskets come with a nonstick coating, cleanup is a breeze. You'll find more time to get out and enjoy an active lifestyle instead of doing dishes. Just be sure to always follow your manufacturer's safety instructions for proper care and cleaning of your air fryer.

Comfort and convenience. Baking with a conventional oven during hot summer months is a surefire way to heat up your whole kitchen in a hurry. It's tempting to turn to a takeaway. But given their compact size, air fryers simply don't give off as much heat. Many models also come with preset features for baking certain types of foods at the press of a button, and some manufacturers now offer air fryers that do double duty as pressure cookers, too. At the end of the day, there are few things that you can make in a conventional oven that you can't make more easily in an air fryer. The only challenge is that sometimes you may need to cook a recipe in batches because the units are obviously smaller. That's simple enough and could even help you stay on track with portions when it comes to making cookies and other dessert batches.

the recipe for weight loss

Every gram of fat and calorie you can cut with the help of your air fryer adds up! Losing weight is a numbers game. Essentially, once you figure out how many calories your body normally burns, make a plan to consume about 500 calories fewer every day and you can look forward to a steady weight loss of a pound a week. There are plenty of online tools to help you calculate your basal metabolic rate (the calories your body needs for basic functions like breathing and keeping your heart beating). These sites also consider your starting size and estimated activity level to help you figure out the total number of calories your body uses.

Keep in mind that the sweet spot for weight loss lies in between your basal metabolic rate and total calories burned in a day.

Severely limiting your calorie intake can actually wreak havoc on your metabolism and cause your body to conserve calories. So make a goal that is realistic, safe, and attainable. Beyond counting calories, these totally manageable strategies can also help power your weight loss.

Focus on fat. One gram of fat contains 9 calories, more than twice the calories you get from 1 gram of protein or carbohydrates, which means that paying careful attention to your ingredients as well as the fats you use in your cooking is a great way to manage your total calorie

HELPFUL KITCHEN TOOLS

In general, you can use any glass, metal, or silicone baking dishes with your air fryer as long as they fit in the basket and don't block the circulation of hot air. Here are some other key items you'll want to have on hand to help you use your air fryer for weight loss:

Kitchen scales: Weighing your food is the best way to make sure your portion sizes stay on track. With digital scales, you can know exactly how big that piece of meat really is.

Olive oil spray: Instead of using nonstick cooking spray, which may over time compromise the integrity of nonstick surfaces, consider purchasing a pump-style spray bottle that you can fill with regular olive oil. Some foods, especially those with a breaded coating, will benefit from a light coating of oil before air frying. If you prefer a neutral-flavoured oil, avocado oil is an excellent choice.

Parchment paper: Treated with a thin layer of silicone, parchment paper provides a nonstick surface for delicate foods that might otherwise slip through the holes of your air fryer basket. When lining your basket with parchment, avoid cutting a piece so large that it covers all the holes (otherwise air will not circulate properly).

Meat thermometer: While the recipes in this collection offer visual hints to explain what your food should look like when it's done, the only way to know for sure whether meats are cooked to a safe temperature is to rely on a meat thermometer.

Tongs: Although it's possible to simply give many foods a quick shake in the basket to ensure even cooking, some foods require deliberate turning. Tongs are helpful for this task.

intake. However, all fats are not created equal. Some, like the monounsaturated fats found in olive oil and nuts, are considered heart-healthy foods because they play an important role in controlling inflammation. In general, try to minimize saturated fats (abundant in red meats and full-fat dairy products). Most experts advise steering clear of trans fats (the kind that manufacturers use in processed foods) altogether.

Don't skimp on protein. Protein is the building block your body needs to build muscle, and it plays an important role in helping to control your appetite and keep your metabolism humming. However, the challenge is that many protein-rich foods are also high in fats, so opt for leaner sources like seafood and poultry whenever feasible. It's also helpful to keep in mind what a healthy serving size looks like. A serving of chicken breast, for example, is about the size of the palm of your hand or a deck of playing cards.

Be careful with carbs. Carbohydrates help your body perform many functions, but where weight loss is concerned it's helpful to think of carbs as a kind of fuel supply that comes in several different grades. Simple carbohydrates (think sugar and white bread) are like low-grade fuel sources that your body burns quickly, which can lead to spikes in both glucose and

hunger levels. Complex carbohydrates, on the other hand, are like a high-grade fuel that your body burns more slowly. Whole grains, fruits, and vegetables are all forms of complex carbohydrates that offer many other valuable nutrients and should be the main source of carbohydrates in a healthy weight loss eating plan.

Get more fibre and drink plenty of water. Complex carbohydrates contain fibre, the indigestible part of plants that keep things moving efficiently through your system. When you're trying to lose weight, fibre is especially beneficial because it helps you feel full longer. Aim for 25 grams of fibre a day. And while you're at it, make sure you're drinking at least 8 glasses of water, too, because dehydration is often the culprit behind the temptation to overeat.

With your air fryer and these smart eating approaches, you can make your favourite foods lighter and weight loss easy. Ready to dig in? Every recipe in the chapters that follow includes nutritional information—calories, fat, protein, and more—to help you stay on track with your goals. And every dish has been designed with your air fryer and weight loss in mind, so eating slimly becomes almost automatic. Start enjoying amazing meals and even luscious desserts while making your way towards a new you—your air fryer is the secret!

good mornings

Small-Batch Granola

Makes 4 servings • Prep time: 10 minutes • Total time: 1 hour 10 minutes

3 tablespoons rapeseed oil

3 tablespoons honey

½ teaspoon vanilla extract

¼ teaspoon ground cinnamon

¼ teaspoon salt

140g porridge oats

30g pecans or walnuts, coarsely chopped

35g raisins or other dried fruit

Your air fryer is golden for making crunchy granola in perfect portions! Going homemade also gives you control of the ingredients and calories—store-bought granola can be loaded with extra sugar and fat. All it takes is 10 minutes of hands-on time while your appliance does the rest to give you a great breakfast that you can take on the go.

1. Preheat the air fryer to 120°C. Cut a piece of parchment paper to fit inside the air fryer basket.

2. In a large bowl, combine the oil, honey, vanilla, cinnamon, and salt. Stir until smooth. Add the oats and nuts and stir until the mixture is thoroughly combined.

3. Spread the oat mixture on the parchment paper to an even thickness.

4. Air fry for 1 hour, or until golden throughout. Remove from the air fryer and allow to fully cool. Break the granola into bite-size pieces if necessary, stir in the raisins, and store in a covered container for up to a week.

TIP: When assembling ingredients, be sure to measure the rapeseed oil first. The little bit of oil remaining in your measuring spoon will ensure the honey slides out easily.

Per 50g serving: 330 calories, 5 g protein, 42 g carbohydrates, 17 g fat (1.5 g sat fat), 4 g fibre

Cherry-Oatmeal Bars

Makes 12 bars • Prep time: 15 minutes • Total time: 50 minutes + cooling time

60g unsalted butter

100g porridge oats

65g plain flour

50g light brown sugar

¼ teaspoon ground ginger

¼ teaspoon coarse salt

140g all-fruit cherry preserve

Enjoy the goodness of oatmeal beyond the bowl! These breakfast bars sandwich luscious fruit filling between two layers of a satisfying crumble crust for a portable breakfast the whole family will love. It's easy to adjust the recipe to your favourite flavour of fruit preserves.

1. Preheat the air fryer to 190°C. Line a 20cm square baking pan with parchment paper so that the paper overhangs two sides like handles.

2. In a large microwave-safe bowl, melt the butter in the microwave on high for 1 minute. Add the oats, flour, brown sugar, ginger, and salt. Stir until thoroughly combined and forms clumps. Set aside 8 tablespoons of the crumble mixture, then press the rest into an even layer in the bottom of the prepared pan.

3. Spread the preserve evenly over the crust. Sprinkle the reserved oat mixture evenly over the top.

4. Air fry the bars for 35 to 40 minutes, until the topping is golden. Place the pan on a wire rack to cool completely before slicing.

TIP: This recipe works best if your air fryer can accommodate a 20cm square pan. If necessary, use a 20cm round pan instead and cut the bars into wedges.

Per bar: 120 calories, 2 g protein, 13 g carbohydrates, 4 g fat (2.5 g sat fat), 1 g fibre

French Toast Cups with Raspberries

Makes 2 servings • Prep time: 15 minutes • Total time: 35 minutes + chilling time

2 slices Italian bread (about 50g), cut into 1cm cubes

60g fresh or frozen raspberries

50g low-fat cream cheese, cut into 5mm cubes

2 large eggs

125ml semi-skimmed milk

3 tablespoons light golden or maple syrup

½ teaspoon vanilla extract

You can have the classic taste of French toast without standing over a hot skillet or breaking the calorie bank. Your air fryer makes it simple! To keep your breakfast slimming, go for light golden or maple pancake syrup. Most brands of light have about half the calories of regular syrup, but you're unlikely to taste much of a difference in this dish because the bright flavour of the raspberries shines through.

1. Coat two 210ml mini pudding basins with nonstick spray.

2. Put one quarter of the bread cubes in each basin. Sprinkle the bread with the raspberries and cream cheese cubes. Top with the remaining bread.

3. In a small bowl, whisk together the eggs, milk, 1 tablespoon of the syrup, and the vanilla. Pour the mixture over the bread. Cover and refrigerate for at least 1 hour.

4. Preheat the air fryer to 160°C. Place the basins in the air fryer basket. Air fry for 12 to 15 minutes, until golden brown and puffed.

5. Serve drizzled with the remaining 2 tablespoons of syrup.

Per serving: 260 calories, 16 g protein, 33 g carbohydrates, 7 g fat (2.8 g sat fat), 3 g fibre

Apple Dutch Baby Pancake

Makes 2 servings • Prep time: 10 minutes • Total time: 55 minutes

30g plain flour

4 tablespoons sugar

¼ teaspoon baking powder

¼ teaspoon ground cinnamon

Pinch of salt

125ml semi-skimmed milk

2 large eggs

½ teaspoon vanilla extract

15g unsalted butter

1 small Granny Smith apple, cored and thinly sliced

2 tablespoons light golden or maple syrup

Turn off the oven and forget simmering apples on the hob, as the traditional version of this recipe usually requires. All of your ingredients for this luscious dish come together easily (and deliciously!) in your air fryer. At 320 calories per serving, it only tastes rich!

1. In a bowl, stir together the flour, 2 tablespoons of the sugar, baking powder, cinnamon, and salt until combined.

2. In a separate bowl, stir together the milk, eggs, and vanilla until combined. Whisk the milk mixture lightly, then slowly add the flour mixture, whisking constantly, until thoroughly combined. Leave the batter to stand for 30 minutes.

3. Preheat the air fryer to 200°C.

4. Place the butter in a 15cm round baking pan and air fry for 1 minute until the butter is melted and the pan is hot.

5. Brush some of the butter up the sides of the pan and sprinkle 1 tablespoon of sugar over the butter. Arrange the apple slices in the pan in a single layer. Sprinkle the remaining 1 tablespoon of sugar over the apples. Air fry for 2 minutes or until the mixture bubbles.

6. Gently pour the batter mixture over the apples. Reduce the air fryer temperature to 180°C and air fry for 12 minutes, or until the batter is golden brown around the edges and the centre is cooked through. Serve drizzled with the pancake syrup.

Per serving: 320 calories, 8 g protein, 57 g carbohydrates, 7 g fat (4.4 g sat fat), 2 g fibre

Cheese, Bacon & Egg Cups

Makes 4 servings • Prep time: 10 minutes • Total time: 22 minutes

4 large eggs

Salt and freshly ground black pepper

50g unsmoked back bacon, chopped

¼ red pepper, seeded and finely chopped

55g reduced-fat Cheddar cheese, grated

1 tablespoon chopped fresh chives (optional)

What's better than an omelette? A medley of favourite breakfast flavours with no pan watching or tricky flipping required! This recipe twist also renders the egg dish perfectly portable for a grab-and-go breakfast. And you have so many options—try adding a different cheese or choice of chopped veggie.

1. Preheat the air fryer to 200°C. Lightly coat 4 silicone muffin cups with vegetable oil.

2. In a bowl, whisk the eggs and season with salt and pepper. Add the bacon, pepper, and half of the cheese. Mix until the ingredients are thoroughly combined. Divide the egg mixture among the muffin cups and top with the remaining cheese.

3. Air fry for 12 to 15 minutes, or until cooked through. Top with fresh chives (if using).

TIP: Silicone baking cups are especially useful to have on hand because they are reusable and offer a little flexibility if space is tight in your air fryer.

Per serving: 130 calories, 13 g protein, 1 g carbohydrates, 8 g fat (3.3 g sat fat), 0 g fibre

Sunny-Side-Up Eggs in Avocado

Makes 2 servings • Prep time: 5 minutes • Total time: 14 minutes

1 Haas avocado, halved and pitted

2 large eggs

Salt and freshly ground black pepper

Chopped fresh parsley, for garnish (optional)

1 lime, cut into wedges (optional)

Avocado toast has won many hearts, but avocado eggs are even more satisfying! The first time you make them, take careful note of how much time your air fryer requires to cook them to the level of doneness that you prefer. Once you've nailed that detail, future batches are a cinch to make. If your menu plan includes carbs, serve with a side of toast.

1. Preheat the air fryer to 200°C.

2. Slice off a thin portion off the rounded bottom of each avocado half so that it will sit solidly in the air fryer basket without rolling around.

3. Break an egg directly into the hollow of each avocado half.

4. Air fry for 9 minutes, pausing halfway through the cooking time to see if the egg whites are set and the yolk has reached the desired doneness.

5. Season to taste with salt and pepper and garnish with chopped parsley (if using). Serve with lime wedges (if using).

Per serving: 185 calories, 8 g protein, 6 g carbohydrates, 15 g fat (3 g sat fat), 5 g fibre

English Muffin Breakfast Pizzas

Makes 2 servings • Prep time: 5 minutes • Total time: 15 minutes

2 whole-grain English muffins, halved horizontally

1 plum tomato, thinly sliced

Salt and freshly ground black pepper

55g reduced-fat firm mozzarella cheese, grated

2 vegetarian breakfast sausages crumbled

Pinch of dried oregano

Craving some cold pizza for breakfast? These toasted breakfast pizzas are a much better choice, loaded with a healthy balance of protein and fibre to get your morning off to a great start. If you need to take your morning meal on the road, simply turn your portion of two mini pizzas into a breakfast sandwich.

1. Preheat the air fryer to 200°C.

2. Arrange the muffin halves cut side up in the air fryer basket. Air fry for 3 minutes until warm.

3. Season the tomato slices to taste with salt and pepper. Set the tomato slices on top of the muffins and scatter equal amounts of cheese and sausage on top, followed by a dash of oregano.

4. Continue air frying for 5 minutes until the cheese is melted and beginning to brown.

Per serving: 285 calories, 21 g protein, 32 g carbohydrates, 9 g fat (3.4 g sat fat), 6 g fibre

Berry Creamy Breakfast Sandwiches

Makes 4 servings • Prep time: 10 minutes • Total time: 15 minutes

115g soft goat's cheese

1 tablespoon honey

8 slices wholewheat bread

130g blackberries

Turn up the flavour and nutrition on your basic jam or marmalade on toast! Blackberries boast an impressive amount of fibre (8 grams per cup), and they work especially well in this toasted sandwich because they hold their shape better than other berries when cooked. Of course, if you're a die-hard fan of another type of berry, feel free to substitute your favourite fruit. The lightly sweetened goat's cheese pairs well with just about everything.

1. Preheat the air fryer to 180°C.

2. In a small bowl, use a fork to mash the goat's cheese and honey into a smooth spread. Divide the cheese mixture among the bread slices and spread evenly almost to the edges.

3. Distribute the berries over 4 slices of bread and top with the remaining slices. Lightly spritz the sandwiches with a neutral-flavoured cooking oil, such as avocado oil.

4. Working in batches if necessary, arrange the sandwiches in the air fryer basket so they are not touching. Air fry for 5 to 7 minutes, or until toasted.

Per serving: 285 calories, 14 g protein, 35 g carbohydrates, 10 g fat (6.1 g sat fat), 4 g fibre

Skinny Chilaquiles

Makes 1 serving • Prep time: 5 minutes • Total time: 15 minutes

3 (15cm) corn tortillas

Pinch of coarse salt

125ml green or red enchilada sauce

1 teaspoon unsalted butter

1 large egg

¼ red onion, thinly sliced

1 tablespoon crumbled feta cheese

Hot sauce, for serving (optional)

Using your air fryer to toast the tortillas is an easy way to prepare this dish with far less oil than if you use regular fried chips. If you have two hungry people in the house, there's no need to prepare a second batch. Just cook another egg and warm up a cup of black beans to share alongside and you'll both enjoy a 310-calorie breakfast instead.

1. Preheat the air fryer to 180°C.

2. Lightly spritz both sides of each tortilla with olive oil and sprinkle with salt. Stack the tortillas and cut into 6 wedges. Scatter the tortillas in the air fryer basket so there is room for the air to circulate. Air fry for 5 minutes, pausing halfway to shake the basket, until the chips begin to brown.

3. Transfer the chips to a large bowl and top with the enchilada sauce, tossing until the chips are thoroughly coated. Return the chips to the air fryer basket and air fry 3 minutes longer until lightly browned.

4. Meanwhile, heat the butter in a small frying pan over medium heat and cook the egg to your desired doneness.

5. Transfer the chips to a plate and top with the egg, onion slices, cheese, and a dash of hot sauce (if using).

Per serving: 385 calories, 14 g protein, 39 g carbohydrates, 20 g fat (9.8 g sat fat), 6 g fibre

Big Easy Sweet Potato Hash

Makes 2 servings • Prep time: 5 minutes • Total time: 15 minutes

1 large sweet potato (350g), peeled and chopped

¼ red onion, chopped

¼ red pepper, seeded and chopped

1 tablespoon olive oil

1 teaspoon Cajun seasoning

85g andouille sausage, or lean Polish sausage, chopped

2 tablespoons chopped fresh parsley

Let the good times roll with the bold flavours in this Cajun version of a classic breakfast hash. With 6 grams of fibre per serving, it's practically guilt-free! If andouille sausage is unavailable, substitute lean Polish sausage in its place. Both work equally well in an air fryer.

1. Preheat the air fryer to 200°C.

2. In a large bowl, combine the sweet potato, onion, and pepper. Drizzle with the oil and sprinkle with the Cajun seasoning. Toss to coat.

3. Transfer the mixture to the air fryer basket and air fry for 10 minutes.

4. Add the sausage and shake the basket. Air fry for 10 minutes longer until the sausage is sizzling and the sweet potatoes are fork-tender and beginning to brown.

5. Top with the parsley before serving.

Per serving: 295 calories, 11 g protein, 37 g carbohydrates, 12 g fat (3 g sat fat), 6 g fibre

Cheese Sausage Biscuit Balls

Makes 6 servings • Prep time: 15 minutes • Total time: 22 minutes

450g lean minced turkey

1 teaspoon salt

1 teaspoon dried sage

½ teaspoon freshly ground black pepper

½ teaspoon onion granules

¼ teaspoon dried chilli flakes (optional)

180g reduced-fat Cheddar cheese, grated

200g scone mix

These tasty breakfast balls are considerably lighter than the popular version you may recall with regular pork sausage and processed cheese. Best of all, if you make a batch ahead of time you can reheat them in the air fryer in a few minutes flat. Perfect for busy mornings!

1. Preheat the air fryer to 200°C.

2. In a large bowl, combine the turkey, salt, sage, black pepper, onion powder, and chilli flakes (if using). Mix gently until thoroughly combined. Add the cheese and scone mix and stir again until combined. Shape the mixture into 3cm balls.

3. Working in batches if necessary, arrange the balls in a single layer in the air fryer basket; spritz lightly with olive oil. Air fry for 7 to 10 minutes, pausing halfway through the cooking time to shake the basket, until lightly browned and a meat thermometer inserted into the centre of a ball reaches 74°C.

TIP: Rubbed sage is dried sage leaves that have been rubbed into a fine, fluffy powder. It's less concentrated so a teaspoon of rubbed sage will be less intense than a teaspoon of ground sage.

Per serving: 350 calories, 27 g protein, 20 g carbohydrates, 18 g fat (7.2 g sat fat), 1 g fibre

quick bites

Fried Cauliflower
with Spicy Dipping Sauce

Makes 4 servings • Prep time: 15 minutes • Total time: 30 minutes

FRIED CAULIFLOWER

300g cauliflower, cut into florets

45g panko breadcrumbs

20g grated Parmesan cheese

1 large egg, beaten

SPICY DIPPING SAUCE

55g light mayonnaise

1 tablespoon sriracha

1 tablespoon lime juice

2 tablespoons chopped fresh coriander (optional)

Deep-fried cauliflower is hard to resist because the crunchy coating and creamy vegetable inside are an unbeatable combination. But just one floret can contain a whopping 200 calories! Fortunately, you can make this treat considerably lighter in calories—and just as delicious—with an air fryer.

1. To make the fried cauliflower: Blanch the cauliflower in boiling water for 2 to 3 minutes. Drain into a colander and rinse with cold water to stop the cooking process. Pat dry with paper towels to remove as much water as possible.

2. In a shallow bowl, combine the breadcrumbs and cheese. Dip each of the florets into the beaten egg, then into the breadcrumb mixture, coating evenly. Arrange the florets in the air fryer basket, making sure they don't touch, and spritz lightly with olive oil. Set the air fryer to 200°C. Working in batches if necessary, air fry for 10 minutes until golden.

3. To make the spicy dipping sauce: Whisk together the mayonnaise, sriracha, and lime juice in a small bowl until smooth. Top with the coriander (if using).

Per serving: 210 calories, 5 g protein, 27 g carbohydrates, 8 g fat (1.7 g sat fat), 3 g fibre

Herbed Ricotta Bites

Makes 4 servings • Prep time: 15 minutes • Total time: 23 minutes + chilling time

225g reduced-fat ricotta cheese

2 tablespoons plain flour

½ teaspoon dried thyme

½ teaspoon dried rosemary, crushed

½ teaspoon dried basil

½ teaspoon coarse salt

¼ teaspoon freshly ground pepper

2 large eggs, beaten

45g panko breadcrumbs

Cheese doesn't need to be off limits! Some research suggests that getting an adequate supply of calcium in your diet can boost your weight loss efforts, which makes cheese dishes like this one even easier to enjoy. However, ricotta has an extremely mild flavour, so perking it up with a good combination of herbs is essential.

1. In a medium bowl, stir together the ricotta, flour, thyme, rosemary, basil, salt, pepper, and half of the beaten eggs until thoroughly combined. Scoop approximately 1 tablespoon of the mixture into the palm of your hand and roll into a ball. Repeat with the remaining mixture.

2. Dip each of the balls into the remaining beaten egg and then into the breadcrumbs, coating evenly.

3. Place the balls on a baking sheet and refrigerate for 1 hour.

4. Preheat the air fryer to 200°C. Spritz the balls lightly with olive oil before transferring to the air fryer basket, making sure they don't touch.

5. Working in batches if necessary, air fry 8 to 9 minutes, or until golden.

Per serving: 210 calories, 9 g protein, 26 g carbohydrates, 5 g fat (3 g sat fat), 0 g fibre

Healthier Mozzarella Sticks

Makes 6 servings • Prep time: 10 minutes • Total time: 16 minutes + freezing time

350g reduced-fat firm mozzarella

70g panko breadcrumbs

20g grated Parmesan cheese

30g plain flour

2 large eggs, beaten

If you enjoy ordering deep-fried mozzarella sticks at your favourite restaurant, this recipe is a game changer. One restaurant serving can contain close to 700 calories! These air-fried mozzarella sticks, on the other hand, come in at less than half that number and are just as appetizing.

1. Cut the cheese into finger-thickness sticks.

2. Place the sticks on a baking sheet, cover with plastic wrap, and freeze for 2 hours.

3. Preheat the air fryer to 200°C.

4. In a shallow bowl, stir together the breadcrumbs and Parmesan cheese. Place the flour and eggs in separate shallow bowls. Roll the frozen cheese in the flour, followed by the eggs, and finally the breadcrumb–Parmesan mixture. Lightly spritz each prepared stick with olive oil.

5. Arrange the sticks in the air fryer basket, making sure they don't touch. Working in batches if necessary, air fry for 3 minutes, then remove and carefully flip. Air fry for an additional 3 to 4 minutes or until golden.

Per serving: 315 calories, 18 g protein, 27 g carbohydrates, 13 g fat (7.8 g sat fat), 0 g fibre

Cabbage Patties with Courgette

Makes 2 servings • Prep time: 20 minutes • Total time: 26 minutes

120g white cabbage, thinly sliced

1 small courgette, grated

1 teaspoon salt

2 spring onions, thinly sliced

1 large egg, beaten

25g panko breadcrumbs

20g grated Parmesan cheese

1 tablespoon chopped fresh dill, plus additional for garnish

55g reduced-fat soured cream

Air fryers are incredibly handy appliances, but they're not the only time-savers in your kitchen. If your food processor has a slicing or shredding disk, you'll definitely want to use it to prep the veggies in this recipe. Cabbage and courgette are both low in fat and high in fibre, making them wonder foods that help you feel full on fewer calories.

1. In a large bowl, combine the cabbage and courgette and sprinkle with the salt. Massage gently until thoroughly combined and leave to stand for 10 minutes. Line a colander with muslin or a clean tea towel and drain the vegetables into the colander. Gather up the sides of the cloth and squeeze gently to remove as much liquid as possible.

2. Preheat the air fryer to 200°C.

3. Place the vegetable mixture back in the bowl and add the spring onions, egg, breadcrumbs, Parmesan, and dill. Mix gently until thoroughly combined. Divide the mixture into 8 equal portions and shape into patties.

4. Arrange the patties in the air fryer basket, making sure they don't touch. Spritz with olive oil. Working in batches if necessary, air fry for 3 minutes, then remove and carefully flip. Air fry for an additional 3 to 4 minutes or until golden.

5. Garnish with fresh dill and serve with the soured cream on the side.

TIP: Allowing the salted vegetables to stand for a few minutes makes it far easier to extract as much water as you can, which will result in firmer patties.

Per serving: 245 calories, 9 g protein, 31 g carbohydrates, 8 g fat (4.5 g sat fat), 3 g fibre

Perfect Steak Fries

Makes 4 servings • Prep time: 5 minutes • Total time: 20 minutes

2 large Maris Piper or Albert Bartlett potatoes, scrubbed and cut into wedges

1 tablespoon olive oil

1 teaspoon coarse salt

½ teaspoon freshly ground black pepper

Chopped fresh thyme, for garnish (optional)

Once you've tasted fries from your air fryer, you'll be hooked! The hot circulating air of the air fryer really helps seal in the flavour of the potato, but the key to crispy success is avoiding an overcrowded basket. Depending on the size of your air fryer, work in batches if necessary.

1. Preheat the air fryer to 200°C.

2. In a large bowl, combine the potatoes, oil, salt, and pepper. Toss until thoroughly coated.

3. Transfer the wedges to the air fryer basket. Air fry for 15 minutes, pausing every 5 minutes to shake the basket, until the fries are golden and crispy.

4. Serve garnished with thyme (if using).

Per serving: 175 calories, 4 g protein, 32 g carbohydrates, 4 g fat (0.5 g sat fat), 3 g fibre

Sweet Onion Rings

Makes 4 servings • Prep time: 15 minutes • Total time: 22 minutes + soaking time

1 large onion, sliced thinly into rounds (about 20 rings)

65g plain flour

½ teaspoon salt, plus extra for seasoning

½ teaspoon baking powder

½ teaspoon freshly ground black pepper

2 large eggs, beaten

45g panko breadcrumbs

Don't think of onion rings as part of a healthy weight loss eating plan? The truth is, your air fryer makes treats like these guilt-free! These healthier rings will not only add significantly less fat to your diet than traditional deep-fried rings, but they're easy to make, too.

1. Soak the onion slices in ice water for 30 minutes to firm them up and seal in their flavour. Drain in a colander.

2. Preheat the air fryer to 200°C.

3. In a shallow bowl, stir together the flour, salt, baking powder, and pepper until combined. Place the eggs and breadcrumbs in separate shallow bowls. Dredge each of the onion rings in the flour mixture, followed by the eggs, and finally the breadcrumbs. Shake off any excess coating and spritz lightly with olive oil.

4. Arrange the onion rings in the air fryer basket, making sure they don't touch. Working in batches if necessary, air fry for 7 minutes, pausing halfway through the cooking time to turn the rings, or until they're golden.

5. Season with additional salt to taste before serving.

Per serving: 175 calories, 3 g protein, 35 g carbohydrates, 1 g fat (0 g sat fat), 1 g fibre

Guilt-Free Veggie Spring Rolls

Makes 4 servings • Prep time: 15 minutes • Total time: 23 minutes

200g crunchy coleslaw vegetable mix

4 spring onions, thinly sliced

2 tablespoons sesame seeds

1 tablespoon reduced-salt soy sauce

1 tablespoon grated fresh ginger

8 spring roll wrappers

1 tablespoon toasted sesame oil

4 tablespoons sweet chilli sauce, for dipping

Using coleslaw is a great shortcut for getting these homemade spring rolls into your air fryer even faster. If you have time, assemble an extra batch to tuck into your freezer. Simply add a few minutes to your cooking time and they can go straight from the freezer into the air fryer.

1. In a large bowl, stir together the coleslaw mix, spring onions, sesame seeds, soy sauce, and ginger until thoroughly combined.

2. To assemble the spring rolls, place a wrapper on a clean, dry surface with one corner facing you. Spoon about 4 tablespoons of the coleslaw mixture evenly onto the wrapper near the bottom corner. Lift this corner up and roll tightly to the middle of the wrapper. Fold the sides in, then continue rolling, tucking in the edges as you go. Dab a small amount of water onto the remaining corner with your fingertip, then press it against the spring roll to seal. Repeat with the remaining wrappers and filling.

3. Brush the spring rolls with the sesame oil and place them in the basket seam-side down, leaving space between them. Air fry at 190°C for 5 to 8 minutes or until golden and crunchy.

4. Serve with the sweet chilli sauce on the side.

Per serving (2 spring rolls): 300 calories, 0 g protein, 48 g carbohydrates, 7 g fat (1 g sat fat), 4 g fibre

Crab Rangoon

Makes 6 servings • Prep time: 15 minutes • Total time: 35 minutes

225g Neufchâtel or Brie cheese, at room temperature

115g white crab meat, drained if canned

2 tablespoons minced spring onion

1 tablespoon reduced-salt soy sauce

30 square wonton wrappers

185ml sweet chilli sauce, for dipping

If weight loss is your goal, ingredients matter. Neufchâtel, for example, has about 30 percent less fat than regular cream cheese. However, cooking methods make a big difference, too, and in this case your air fryer is saving you about 16 grams of fat per serving compared to a deep-fried version.

1. Preheat the air fryer to 180°C.

2. In a bowl, combine the Neufchâtel, crab meat, spring onion, and soy sauce and mix until thoroughly combined.

3. Working with one wrapper at a time, place a teaspoon of filling in the centre of the wonton. Use your finger to moisten the edges of the wonton with warm water to form a sticky surface, and then lift the opposite corners up to meet in the centre, pressing gently to seal. Seal the edges of the dumpling, pressing out as much air as you can.

4. Arrange the dumplings in the air fryer basket so they don't touch and spritz lightly with olive oil. Air fry for 6 minutes until crisp and golden.

5. Serve with the sweet chilli sauce on the side.

Per serving: 300 calories, 11 g protein, 42 g carbohydrates, 9 g fat (5 g sat fat), 2 g fibre

Bacon-Wrapped Asparagus

Makes 4 servings • Prep time: 10 minutes • Total time: 20 minutes

8 slices reduced-salt bacon, cut in half

16 thick asparagus spears (about 450g), trimmed of woody ends

1 lemon, cut into wedges

There are few foods that don't taste better wrapped in bacon, and asparagus is hardly the exception. An added bonus: the circulating heat of your air fryer ensures that each piece is evenly browned.

1. Preheat the air fryer to 180°C.

2. Wrap a half piece of bacon around the centre of each stalk of asparagus.

3. Working in batches, if necessary, arrange seam-side down in a single layer in the air fryer basket. Air fry for 10 minutes until the bacon is crisp and the stalks are tender.

4. Serve with lemon wedges.

TIP: If large asparagus spears aren't available, wrap each piece of bacon around two or three thinner spears.

Per serving: 130 calories, 10 g protein, 5 g carbohydrates, 9 g fat (2.5 g sat fat), 2 g fibre

Smoky Chickpeas

Makes 4 servings • Prep time: 5 minutes • Total time: 25 minutes

400g can chickpeas, rinsed and drained

1 tablespoon olive oil

2 teaspoons lime juice

½ teaspoon salt

½ teaspoon smoked paprika

½ teaspoon garlic powder

Be forewarned—these crispy chickpeas are addictive! But you can feel good knowing that they're packed with protein and fibre. Enjoy them on their own, as a topping for salads, or a great crunchy addition to a wrap or sandwich.

1. Preheat the air fryer to 190°C.

2. Place the chickpeas in the air fryer basket and air fry for 15 minutes, pausing a few times to shake the basket, until the chickpeas are dry and beginning to crisp.

3. Meanwhile, in a large bowl, stir together the olive oil, lime juice, salt, paprika, and garlic powder until combined. Carefully transfer the chickpeas to the bowl and use a silicone spatula to stir until the chickpeas are thoroughly coated.

4. Return the seasoned chickpeas to the air fryer basket and reduce the temperature to 175°C. Air fry for 2 to 3 minutes longer until crisp.

5. The chickpeas will become crunchy as they cool. Serve at room temperature. Store in an airtight container for 3 to 5 days.

TIP: Cooking the chickpeas first until they dry ensures the seasonings remain flavourful.

Per serving: 160 calories, 7 g protein, 22 g carbohydrates, 6 g fat (1 g sat fat), 6 g fibre

Crispy Tofu Bites

Makes 4 servings • Prep time: 5 minutes • Total time: 20 minutes

450g extra-firm tofu, drained and pressed

1 tablespoon olive oil

2 teaspoons dry barbecue seasoning

½ teaspoon salt

125ml barbecue sauce

The key to great-tasting tofu is to make sure you press as much liquid out of it as possible before cooking so that it absorbs flavours well. In this super-simple recipe, you can season the tofu right on your cutting board and massage it gently with your hands before transferring it to your air fryer. Serve with pickled cucumber slices.

1. Preheat the air fryer to 190°C.

2. Slice the tofu into 2.5cm cubes, drizzle with the olive oil, and sprinkle with the barbecue seasoning and salt. Toss gently with your hands until the cubes are completely coated.

3. Arrange the tofu in a single layer in your air fryer basket. Air fry for 10 to 15 minutes, pausing every 5 minutes to shake the basket, until the tofu begins to brown and crisp at the edges.

4. Carefully transfer the tofu to a large bowl and top with the barbecue sauce. Use a silicone spatula to toss gently until thoroughly coated.

Per serving: *200 calories, 11 g protein, 18 g carbohydrates, 9 g fat (1.2 g sat fat), 2 g fibre*

weeknight dinners

California-Style Turkey Burgers

Makes 4 servings • Prep time: 10 minutes • Total time: 25 minutes

450g lean minced turkey

1 tablespoon Dijon mustard

1 tablespoon reduced-fat mayonnaise

Salt and freshly ground black pepper

4 hamburger buns with sesame seeds

4 slices low-fat Monterey Jack cheese

½ carrot, grated

A small handful of baby spinach

1 large tomato, thinly sliced

You may never have considered shredded carrots to be an essential sandwich ingredient, but it's an easy way to add a sweet little crunch to your burgers. And there's no need for added condiments when mustard and mayonnaise are already incorporated into the patties to keep them juicy in the air fryer.

1. Preheat the air fryer to 180°C.

2. In a large bowl, stir together the turkey, Dijon, and mayonnaise. Season with salt and pepper. Mix until thoroughly combined, then divide the mixture and shape into 4 patties.

3. Arrange the patties in the air fryer basket so they are not touching. Air fry for 15 minutes, pausing halfway through the cooking time to flip the burgers, until browned and the temperature in the thickest portion is 74°C.

4. Place the patties on the buns and top with the cheese, carrot, spinach, and tomato slices before serving.

Per serving: 380 calories, 33 g protein, 22 g carbohydrates, 19 g fat (7 g sat fat), 4 g fibre

Thai Chicken Skewers with Peanut Sauce

Makes 4 servings • Prep time: 15 minutes • Total time: 25 minutes + marinating time

CHICKEN SKEWERS

2 tablespoons Thai red curry paste

2 tablespoons rapeseed oil

1 tablespoon lime juice

2 cloves garlic, minced

680g boneless, skinless chicken breasts, cut into fingers

PEANUT SAUCE

75g creamy peanut butter

Juice of ½ lime

1 tablespoon reduced-salt soy sauce

1 teaspoon brown sugar

1 teaspoon grated fresh ginger

1 teaspoon chilli-garlic sauce

60ml water

There are so many ways to enjoy this chicken dish! Serve the seasoned chicken with brown rice, noodles, or cucumber salad, or load it into a whole-grain wrap with your favourite crisp veggies.

1. To make the chicken skewers: In a small bowl, whisk together the curry paste, oil, lime juice, and garlic until smooth. Transfer the mixture to a large resealable bag. Add the chicken, seal the bag, and massage the bag to ensure the chicken is evenly coated. Refrigerate for 1 hour (or up to 8 hours).

2. To make the peanut sauce: In a medium bowl, whisk together the peanut butter, lime juice, soy sauce, brown sugar, ginger, and chilli-garlic sauce until combined. Slowly add the water and whisk until smooth. Cover and refrigerate until ready to use.

3. To finish the dish, preheat the air fryer to 200°C.

4. Discard the marinade and thread the chicken back and forth onto metal skewers that fit in your air fryer. Working in batches if necessary, air fry the skewers for 10 to 12 minutes until cooked through, pausing halfway through the time to turn the skewers and lightly baste with a few tablespoons of the peanut sauce.

5. Serve with the remaining peanut sauce for dipping.

TIP: Covered and refrigerated, the peanut sauce will easily keep for up to a week.

Per serving: 410 calories, 45 g protein, 8 g carbohydrates, 23 g fat (4 g sat fat), 1 g fibre

Tandoori Chicken with Cucumber Raita

Makes 4 servings • Prep time: 10 minutes • Total time: 25 minutes + marinating time

215g natural nonfat Greek yogurt, divided

2 cloves garlic, minced

1 tablespoon grated fresh ginger

½ teaspoon ground cayenne

½ teaspoon ground turmeric

½ teaspoon garam masala

1 teaspoon ground cumin

1 teaspoon salt, plus extra to season

680g boneless, skinless chicken breasts

1 small cucumber, peeled and grated

1 small carrot, peeled and grated

1 lemon, cut into 6 wedges

2 tablespoons chopped fresh mint

2 tablespoons chopped fresh coriander

½ onion, sliced

A tandoor is a traditional clay oven that cooks food quickly at very high heat and is used throughout many parts of the Middle East and Asia. While your air fryer won't be able to match those temperatures, the convenience it affords is the next best thing. Serve with brown basmati rice.

1. In a small bowl, whisk 55g of the yogurt with the garlic, ginger, cayenne, turmeric, garam masala, cumin, and salt until smooth.

2. Transfer the yogurt mixture to a large resealable bag. Add the chicken, seal the bag, and massage the bag to ensure the chicken is evenly coated. Refrigerate for 1 hour (or up to 8 hours).

3. Preheat the air fryer to 180°C.

4. Remove the chicken from the marinade (discard the marinade) and arrange in a single layer in the air fryer basket. Air fry for 15 to 20 minutes, pausing halfway through the cooking time to flip the chicken, until a meat thermometer inserted into the thickest part reaches 74°C.

5. Meanwhile, prepare the raita. In a bowl, combine the remaining yogurt with the cucumber, carrot, juice of 2 lemon wedges, and mint. Season to taste with salt.

6. Garnish the chicken with the coriander. Serve the chicken alongside the raita, remaining 4 lemon wedges, and sliced onion.

Per serving: 240 calories, 45 g protein, 5 g carbohydrates, 4 g fat (1.3 g sat fat), 1 g fibre

Caribbean Chicken with Mango Salsa

Makes 4 servings • Prep time: 15 minutes • Total time: 30 minutes

CARIBBEAN CHICKEN

2 tablespoons brown sugar

1 tablespoon ground allspice

1 teaspoon salt

1 teaspoon cumin

1 teaspoon dried thyme

½ teaspoon cayenne pepper (optional)

680g boneless, skinless chicken breasts

1 tablespoon olive oil

MANGO SALSA

1 large mango, peeled and diced

¼ red pepper, seeded and finely diced

2 spring onions, finely chopped

Juice of ½ lime

2 tablespoons chopped fresh coriander

¼ teaspoon salt

If you have the time, prep these spice-rubbed chicken breasts and pop them into a resealable bag in your fridge overnight. The flavours will only improve. However, if time is tight, this spice rub can work magic in the air fryer without that extra step.

1. Preheat the air fryer to 180°C.

2. To make the chicken: In a small bowl, stir together the brown sugar, allspice, salt, cumin, thyme, and cayenne (if using) until combined. Rub the chicken breasts with the spice mixture until thoroughly coated and then drizzle with the olive oil.

3. Arrange the chicken in a single layer in the air fryer basket. Air fry for 15 to 20 minutes, pausing halfway through the cooking time to flip the chicken, until a meat thermometer inserted into the thickest part reaches 74°C.

4. Meanwhile, to make the mango salsa: In a large bowl, combine the mango, pepper, spring onions, lime juice, coriander, and salt.

5. Serve the chicken topped with the mango salsa.

Per serving: 305 calories, 40 g protein, 21 g carbohydrates, 8 g fat (1.8 g sat fat), 2 g fibre

Chicken Fajitas

Makes 4 servings • Prep time: 15 minutes • Total time: 30 minutes

450g boneless, skinless chicken breasts, cut into fingers

½ onion, thinly sliced

½ red pepper, seeded and thinly sliced

½ green pepper, seeded and thinly sliced

1 tablespoon vegetable oil

1 tablespoon fajita seasoning

1 teaspoon coarse salt

Juice of ½ lime

8 small flour tortillas

115g prepared guacamole

It's time to reimagine family taco night! You don't need beef, cheese, and fried taco shells to create a fiesta when your air fryer can help you get an alternative dish on the table quickly. These easy chicken fajitas are every bit as delicious and far easier to fit into a healthy weight loss plan.

1. Preheat the air fryer to 200°C.

2. In a large bowl, combine the chicken, onion, and peppers. Drizzle with the vegetable oil and toss until thoroughly coated. Add the fajita seasoning and salt and toss again.

3. Working in batches if necessary, arrange the chicken and vegetables in a single layer in the air fryer basket. Air fry for 15 minutes, pausing halfway through the cooking time to shake the basket, until the vegetables are tender and the chicken is cooked through.

4. Transfer the mixture to a serving platter and drizzle with the fresh lime juice.

5. Place the chicken mixture on the tortillas and serve with the guacamole.

Per serving: *410 calories, 32 g protein, 37 g carbohydrates, 15 g fat (3.1 g sat fat), 5 g fibre*

General Tso's Chicken

Makes 4 servings • Prep time: 10 minutes • Total time: 25 minutes

4 boneless, skinless chicken thighs (about 550g)

Salt and freshly ground black pepper

2 tablespoons cornflour

2 tablespoons rice vinegar

2 tablespoons reduced-salt soy sauce

2 teaspoons hoisin sauce

2 tablespoons sugar

2 cloves garlic, minced

1 teaspoon sriracha (optional)

2 spring onions, thinly sliced

1 tablespoon sesame seeds

While you'll never find this dish if you happen to travel to China, it's a popular takeaway dish. Most deep-fried versions rely on cornflour to help make the chicken extra crispy. Fortunately, with an air fryer you can get similar results but skip the added fat and calories.

1. Preheat the air fryer to 200°C.

2. Cut the chicken into bite-size pieces and place in a large bowl. Season with salt and pepper. Sprinkle with the cornflour and toss to coat.

3. Spread the chicken in the air fryer basket in a single layer and spritz lightly with olive oil. Air fry for 15 minutes, pausing halfway through the cooking time to shake the basket, until the chicken is cooked through.

4. Meanwhile, in another large bowl, whisk together the vinegar, soy sauce, hoisin sauce, sugar, garlic, and sriracha (if using). Transfer the cooked chicken to the bowl and toss to coat.

5. Top with the spring onions and sesame seeds before serving.

Per serving: 270 calories, 28 g protein, 17 g carbohydrates, 10 g fat (2.9 g sat fat), 1 g fibre

Chinese Chicken Patties

Makes 4 servings • Prep time: 10 minutes • Total time: 20 minutes

680g extra-lean minced chicken

225g can water chestnuts, drained and chopped

3 tablespoons hoisin sauce

3 spring onions, thinly sliced

1 tablespoon grated fresh ginger

These five-ingredient chicken patties are quick to put together and so very versatile. Serve with brown rice and steamed vegetables, or if you are watching your carb intake, try them in lettuce cups.

1. Preheat the air fryer to 200°C.

2. In a large bowl, stir together the chicken, water chestnuts, hoisin sauce, spring onions, and ginger until thoroughly combined. Shape into 8 patties, each about 1cm thick.

3. Arrange the patties in a single layer in the air fryer basket. Spritz lightly with olive oil. Air fry for 10 minutes, or until the temperature in the thickest portion of the patty registers 74°C.

Per serving: 240 calories, 36 g protein, 12 g carbohydrates, 6 g fat (1 g sat fat), 2 g fibre

Chicken Cobb Salad with Buffalo Drizzle

Makes 4 servings • Prep time: 20 minutes • Total time: 35 minutes

2 boneless, skinless chicken breasts (about 450g)

Salt and freshly ground black pepper

2 tablespoons unsalted butter

2 tablespoons hot sauce

2 tablespoons olive oil

2 teaspoons cider vinegar

1 small cos lettuce, chopped

2 hard-boiled eggs, chopped

25g blue cheese, crumbled

100g cherry tomatoes, chopped

½ small red onion, chopped

1 avocado, halved, pitted, and chopped

Spice up a classic combination of Cobb salad ingredients with a rich drizzle of buttery hot sauce! If you're a big Buffalo wing fan, this zesty chicken salad is sure to please your taste buds while helping you stay on track with smart eating.

1. Preheat the air fryer to 190°C.

2. Season the chicken breasts with salt and pepper. Spritz lightly with olive oil spray. Arrange the chicken in a single layer in the air fryer basket. Air fry for 15 to 20 minutes, pausing halfway through the cooking time to flip the chicken, until a meat thermometer inserted into the thickest part reaches 74°C.

3. Meanwhile, in a large microwave-safe bowl, melt the butter in the microwave on high for 1 minute. Whisk in the hot sauce and set aside.

4. In another large bowl, whisk together the olive oil and vinegar until thoroughly combined. Season to taste with salt and pepper. Add the lettuce and toss to coat. Arrange the eggs, blue cheese, tomatoes, red onion, and avocado on top.

5. When the chicken is cool enough to handle, slice into thin pieces or chop into bite-size pieces and add to the butter mixture. Toss until the chicken is thoroughly coated. Top the salad with the chicken and drizzle any sauce that remains on top.

Per serving: 395 calories, 33 g protein, 7 g carbohydrates, 26 g fat (8.2 g sat fat), 4 g fibre

Asian Pork Salad

Makes 4 servings • Prep time: 20 minutes • Total time: 30 minutes + marinating time

Juice of 1 lime

2 tablespoons reduced-salt soy sauce

1 tablespoon fish sauce

2 tablespoons toasted sesame oil

1 tablespoon lemongrass paste (optional)

450g pork loin, trimmed and thinly sliced

225g vermicelli rice noodles

½ onion, thinly sliced

2 spring onions. chopped

2 carrots, grated

1 cucumber, julienned

½ small cos lettuce, sliced

Salt

4 small sprigs fresh mint

2 shallots, chopped and fried (optional)

If you love Asian food, keep this satisfying salad in your regular dinner rotation for its speed and convenience. Once the pork has marinated, this dish only requires about 10 minutes in the air fryer, which is plenty of time to cook the noodles and prep the rest of the vegetables.

1. In a large bowl, whisk together the lime juice, soy sauce, fish sauce, 1 tablespoon of the sesame oil, and lemongrass paste (if using). Add the pork and toss until thoroughly coated. Leave to stand at room temperature for 30 minutes or cover and refrigerate overnight.

2. Preheat the air fryer to 200°C.

3. Spread the pork in a single layer in the air fryer basket. Air fry for 10 minutes, pausing halfway through the cooking time to turn the meat, until cooked through and the edges begin to crisp.

4. Meanwhile, prepare the vermicelli according to the package instructions and rinse the noodles under cold water to stop the cooking process. Transfer the noodles to another large bowl and toss with the remaining 1 tablespoon of sesame oil.

5. Arrange the noodles, onion, spring onions, carrot, cucumber, and lettuce in bowls. Season to taste with salt. Serve topped with the pork, fresh mint, and shallots (if using).

Per serving: 535 calories, 37 g protein, 53 g carbohydrates, 19 g fat (5 g sat fat), 2 g fibre

Easy Weeknight Pork Kebabs

Makes 4 servings • Prep time: 15 minutes • Total time: 25 minutes

60ml orange juice

2 tablespoons honey

2 tablespoons Worcestershire sauce

1 tablespoon olive oil

1 large clove garlic, minced

2 peppers, preferably red or orange

1 pork tenderloin (about 550g)

Trimming a pork tenderloin into small bite-size cubes means it will cook even faster in your air fryer, and sandwiching chunks of pepper in between the meat helps all the flavours combine as the kebabs roast. Feel free to add some onions or courgette to the mix if you prefer, but this simple combination helps you save time with delicious results.

1. In a large bowl, whisk together the orange juice, honey, Worcestershire sauce, olive oil, and garlic.

2. Cut the tops off the peppers, remove the seeds, and cut each pepper into 8 equal pieces. Slice the pork into 16 equal pieces. Transfer the peppers and pork to the bowl with the marinade mixture and toss until thoroughly coated.

3. Preheat the air fryer to 200°C.

4. Thread the pork and peppers onto 4 metal skewers that will fit inside the air fryer basket. Arrange the kebabs in the air fryer basket so they are not touching and air fry for 10 to 12 minutes, pausing halfway through the cooking time to flip the kebabs, until a meat thermometer inserted into the thickest portion reaches 63°C.

Per serving: 250 calories, 31 g protein, 16 g carbohydrates, 7 g fat (1.5 g sat fat), 1 g fibre

Chicken Parmigiana

Makes 4 servings • Prep time: 10 minutes • Total time: 28 minutes

2 large boneless, skinless chicken breasts (about 550g)

Salt and freshly ground black pepper

45g panko breadcrumbs

40g grated Parmesan cheese

2 teaspoons Italian seasoning

1 large egg, lightly beaten

250g tomato and herb pasta sauce

50g fresh mozzarella, sliced

2 tablespoons chopped fresh basil

What started as a riff on a traditional way to serve aubergine has become a favourite beyond Italy. Fortunately, you don't have to forego this beloved and tasty classic when you have an air fryer to help you slash unnecessary calories from the finished dish.

1. Preheat the air fryer to 180°C.

2. Slice the chicken breasts in half horizontally to create 4 thinner chicken breasts. Working with one piece at a time, place the chicken between two pieces of parchment paper and pound with a meat mallet or rolling pin to flatten to an even thickness. Season both sides with salt and pepper.

3. In a large shallow bowl, stir together the breadcrumbs, Parmesan, and Italian seasoning until thoroughly combined. Place the egg in another large shallow bowl. Dip the chicken in the egg, followed by the breadcrumb mixture, pressing firmly to create an even coating.

4. Working in batches if necessary, arrange the chicken breasts in a single layer in the air fryer basket and coat both sides lightly with vegetable oil. Pausing halfway through the cooking time to flip the chicken, air fry for 15 minutes, or until a meat thermometer inserted into the thickest part reaches 74°C.

5. Spoon the sauce over each piece of chicken and top with the mozzarella cheese. Air fry for an additional 3 to 5 minutes until the cheese is melted.

6. Garnish with the basil before serving.

Per serving: 410 calories, 44 g protein, 28 g carbohydrates, 9 g fat (4.9 g sat fat), 2 g fibre

Favourite Lemon Chicken

4 boneless, skinless chicken breasts (about 680g)

1 tablespoon olive oil

1½ teaspoons lemon-pepper seasoning, or grated zest of 1 lemon and extra pepper to season

½ teaspoon paprika

½ teaspoon garlic powder

¼ teaspoon dried oregano

¼ teaspoon freshly ground black pepper

Juice of ½ lemon

To save time later in the week, prepare a double batch of this chicken. It will surely get gobbled up! Leftover cooked chicken breast is a great source of lean protein and a lifesaver for tossing into pasta dishes, on top of salads, or in sandwiches or wraps.

1. Preheat the air fryer to 180°C.

2. Place the chicken in a large bowl and drizzle with the olive oil. Top with the lemon-pepper seasoning, paprika, garlic powder, oregano, and pepper. Toss until thoroughly coated.

3. Working in batches if necessary, arrange the chicken in a single layer in the air fryer basket. Air fry for 20 to 25 minutes, pausing halfway through the cooking time to turn the chicken, until a meat thermometer inserted into the thickest piece reaches 74°C.

4. Transfer the chicken to a serving platter and squeeze the lemon juice over the top.

Per serving: 225 calories, 39 g protein, 0 g carbohydrates, 7 g fat (1.7 g sat fat), 0 g fibre

Simply Terrific Turkey Meatballs

Makes 4 servings • Prep time: 10 minutes • Total time: 20 minutes

¼ onion

2 cloves garlic, coarsely chopped

4 tablespoons coarsely chopped fresh parsley

450g lean minced turkey

1 large egg, lightly beaten

35g panko breadcrumbs

1 teaspoon salt

½ teaspoon freshly ground black pepper

Finely chopped onion, garlic, and parsley add both moisture and flavour to these juicy meatballs. Pair them with pasta and a herby tomato sauce or load them into a meatball sandwich. However you serve them, they'll be a hit every time!

1. Preheat the air fryer to 200°C.

2. In a food processor fitted with a metal blade, pulse the onion, garlic, and parsley until finely chopped. Transfer the vegetables to a large mixing bowl.

3. Add the turkey, egg, breadcrumbs, salt, and pepper. Mix gently until thoroughly combined. Shape the mixture into 3cm meatballs.

4. Working in batches if necessary, arrange the meatballs in a single layer in the air fryer basket; spritz lightly with olive oil. Air fry for 7 to 10 minutes, pausing halfway through the cooking time to shake the basket, until lightly browned and a meat thermometer inserted into the centre of a meatball reaches 74°C.

Per serving: 300 calories, 23 g protein, 16 g carbohydrates, 14 g fat (3.5 g sat fat), 0 g fibre

Greek Meatballs
with Tzatziki Sauce

Makes 4 servings • Prep time: 10 minutes • Total time: 20 minutes

GREEK MEATBALLS

450g lean minced chicken

1 large egg

4 cloves garlic, grated

2 teaspoons dried oregano

1 teaspoon dried thyme

1 teaspoon lemon zest

Salt and freshly ground black pepper

TZATZIKI SAUCE

215g nonfat natural Greek yogurt

½ cucumber, grated

1 tablespoon fresh lemon juice

1 clove garlic, grated

½ teaspoon salt

4 (15cm) pitas

Lettuce for garnish

When you're hankering for a tasty Greek meal, let your kitchen tools save the day. Your air fryer will slash calories and fat without sacrificing flavour. A Microplane grater, the same tool you use to grate the lemon zest, ensures garlicky goodness with every bite.

1. Preheat the air fryer to 200°C.

2. To make the meatballs: In a large bowl, stir together the chicken, egg, garlic, oregano, thyme, and lemon zest. Season with salt and pepper. Mix gently until thoroughly combined. Shape the mixture into 3cm meatballs.

3. Working in batches if necessary, arrange the meatballs in a single layer in the air fryer basket; spritz lightly with olive oil. Air fry for 7 to 10 minutes, pausing halfway through the cooking time to shake the basket, until lightly browned and a meat thermometer inserted into the centre of a meatball reaches 74°C.

4. To make the tzatziki sauce: Stir together the yogurt, cucumber, lemon juice, garlic, and salt in a small bowl until thoroughly combined.

5. Serve the meatballs with the lettuce in the pita bread and top with the tzatziki sauce.

Per serving: 345 calories, 37 g protein, 38 g carbohydrates, 5 g fat (0.8 g sat fat), 2 g fibre

Pork Tenderloin with Apricot Glaze

Makes 4 servings • Prep time: 10 minutes • Total time: 28 minutes

100g apricot preserve

1 tablespoon Dijon mustard

1 pork tenderloin (about 450g)

2 teaspoons olive oil

½ teaspoon dried thyme

½ teaspoon salt

¼ teaspoon freshly ground black pepper

Lean pork tenderloin pairs so perfectly with a sweet apricot glaze! And with 24 grams of protein for only 205 calories, this dish is sure to become one of your air fryer favourites.

1. Preheat the air fryer to 180°C.

2. In a small bowl, stir together the preserve and Dijon and mix until thoroughly combined. Set aside.

3. Rub the pork with the olive oil, thyme, salt, and pepper. Arrange the pork in the air fryer basket. Air fry for 18 to 20 minutes, pausing halfway through the cooking time to turn the pork and brush with half the glaze, until a meat thermometer inserted into the thickest portion reaches 63°C. Brush again with the remaining glaze 2 to 3 minutes before the pork is done.

4. Leave the pork to rest for 5 minutes before slicing.

TIP: If necessary, cut the tenderloin into two pieces so that it fits easily in your air fryer basket.

Per serving: 205 calories, 24 g protein, 16 g carbohydrates, 5 g fat (1.1 g sat fat), 0 g fibre

Cuban Tenderloin

Makes 4 servings • Prep time: 10 minutes • Total time: 30 minutes + marinating time

1 pork tenderloin (about 450g)

125ml orange juice

Juice of 1 lime

1 tablespoon olive oil

2 teaspoons ground cumin

6 cloves garlic, chopped

½ teaspoon salt

¼ teaspoon freshly ground black pepper

4 tablespoons chopped fresh coriander

Once you account for the marinating time, this dish goes from the air fryer to the table with incredible ease. To boost your fibre intake, serve with black beans and brown rice. And if you are lucky enough to have leftovers, they're a perfect main ingredient for a Cuban sandwich; just add some deli ham, mustard, Swiss cheese, and pickles.

1. In a large resealable bag, combine the pork, orange juice, lime juice, olive oil, cumin, garlic, salt, and pepper. Massage lightly to coat the pork. Refrigerate for 4 hours or overnight.

2. Preheat the air fryer to 180°C.

3. Remove the pork from the marinade and discard the marinade. Arrange the pork in the air fryer basket and spritz lightly with olive oil. Air fry for 18 to 20 minutes, pausing halfway through the cooking time to turn the pork, until a meat thermometer inserted into the thickest portion reaches 63°C.

4. Let the pork rest for 5 minutes before slicing. Serve topped with the coriander.

Per serving: 140 calories, 24 g protein, 2 g carbohydrates, 4 g fat (1 g sat fat), 0 g fibre

Garlic Rosemary Pork Chops with Roasted Asparagus

Makes 2 servings • Prep time: 10 minutes • Total time: 20 minutes

225g asparagus spears

Salt and freshly ground black pepper

2 pork chops (about 350g)

1 teaspoon olive oil

2 cloves garlic, minced

1 teaspoon Italian seasoning

2 tablespoons pesto

2 rosemary sprigs, for garnish

This easy, low-carb version of a one-dish meal for your air fryer is sure to win rave reviews. It comes together quickly, so if you're serving more than two people, simply cook in batches.

1. Preheat the air fryer to 190°C.

2. Snap the ends off the asparagus. Spritz lightly with olive oil and season to taste with salt and pepper. Set aside.

3. Drizzle the pork chops with the olive oil and top with the garlic, Italian seasoning, salt, and pepper. Rub the pork chops until thoroughly coated with the seasonings, then arrange the chops in the air fryer basket so that they are not touching.

4. Cook for 10 to 12 minutes, pausing halfway through the cooking time to turn the pork chops and add the asparagus, until a meat thermometer inserted into the thickest portion of a chop reaches 63°C and the asparagus is tender. Leave to rest for 5 minutes.

5. Serve topped with the pesto and the rosemary.

Per serving: 250 calories, 25 g protein, 6 g carbohydrates, 15 g fat (3.3 g sat fat), 2 g fibre

Ham and Cheese Calzones

Makes 4 servings • Prep time: 10 minutes • Total time: 20 minutes

2 tablespoons plain flour

350g pizza dough, divided into 4 equal pieces

225g deli ham

120g reduced-fat firm mozzarella cheese, grated

½ small red onion, finely chopped

2 teaspoons olive oil, divided

250g tomato and herb pasta sauce

Most supermarkets sell packs of premade pizza dough either fresh or frozen, which makes these delicious calzones super easy to put together in an air fryer. You'll likely need a kitchen scale to measure out a smaller portion for this recipe, but the unused dough will keep well for several days in your refrigerator. Do not refreeze dough that has been thawed.

1. Preheat the air fryer to 180°C.

2. Lightly dust your work surface with the flour, then stretch each piece of pizza dough into a thin circle. Divide the ham, cheese, and red onion on one half of each circle of dough. Fold the opposite side over the top to form semicircles. Pinch the edges closed or press with a fork. Brush each calzone lightly with ½ teaspoon of olive oil.

3. Working in batches if necessary, arrange the calzones in the air fryer basket. Air fry for 10 minutes or until lightly browned.

4. Meanwhile, place the pasta sauce in a microwave-safe bowl and heat for 1 minute on high until warm. Serve with the calzones.

Per serving: 425 calories, 24 g protein, 49 g carbohydrates, 14 g fat (4.8 g sat fat), 3 g fibre

Korean Beef in Lettuce Cups

Makes 4 servings • Prep time: 20 minutes • Total time: 30 minutes + marinating time

2 tablespoons gochujang (Korean chilli paste)

2 cloves garlic, minced

2 teaspoons grated fresh ginger

1 tablespoon toasted sesame oil

1 tablespoon reduced-salt soy sauce

1 tablespoon sesame seeds

2 teaspoons sugar

½ teaspoon salt

450g beef sirloin, thinly sliced and trimmed of visible fat

1 small red onion, thinly sliced

2 Little Gem lettuces, leaves separated into "cups"

4 spring onions, thinly sliced

150g kimchi

Traditional Korean bulgogi, a delicious Asian barbecue specialty, is usually made with beef rib eye. However, if weight loss is your goal, you can turn to a leaner cut, like sirloin, that will work nicely in the air fryer. Both gochujang and kimchi come in varying degrees of spiciness, so choose the heat level you prefer.

1. In a small bowl, whisk together the gochujang, garlic, ginger, sesame oil, soy sauce, sesame seeds, sugar, and salt. Place the beef and onions in a resealable bag along with the marinade and massage gently until thoroughly coated. Leave to stand at room temperature for 30 minutes or refrigerate for up to 24 hours.

2. Preheat the air fryer to 200°C.

3. Transfer the meat and onions to the air fryer basket, leaving behind as much of the marinade as possible and spreading the meat in an even layer. Discard the marinade. Air fry for 10 minutes, pausing halfway through the cooking time to turn the meat, until browned and cooked through.

4. To serve, divide the beef and onions among the lettuce cups and top with the spring onions and kimchi.

Per serving: *280 calories, 29 g protein, 8 g carbohydrates, 14 g fat (4.6 g sat fat), 3 g fibre*

Stuffed Peppers

Makes 4 servings • Prep time: 15 minutes • Total time: 47 minutes

450g lean minced beef

½ onion, chopped

4 peppers, tops and seeds removed

250g pack microwave-ready quinoa and brown rice

80g canned chopped tomatoes

2 tablespoons chopped fresh parsley

¾ teaspoon salt

¼ teaspoon freshly ground black pepper

90g reduced-fat Cheddar cheese, grated

A package of ready-to-heat quinoa and brown rice helps boost both the fibre and the protein in this dish while still meeting all the requirements of a tried-and-true family favourite. An added bonus is that you can take advantage of all the peppers available in late summer and enjoy real comfort food without turning on the oven.

1. Preheat the air fryer to 200°C.

2. Crumble the beef into a single layer in the air fryer basket. Scatter the onion on top. Air fry for 15 to 20 minutes until the beef is browned and cooked through.

3. Meanwhile, arrange the peppers in a microwave-safe dish and cover loosely with parchment paper or plastic wrap. Microwave on high for 2 to 3 minutes until the peppers begin to soften.

4. To assemble the peppers, carefully transfer the beef and onions to a large mixing bowl. Use the side of a spoon to break up any large pieces of beef. Drain the grease and wash the air fryer basket. Turn the air fryer down to 180°C.

5. To the beef mixture, add the quinoa and rice, tomatoes, parsley, salt, and pepper. Stir gently until thoroughly combined.

6. Divide the mixture among the peppers and arrange cut-side up in the air fryer basket. Air fry for 15 to 20 minutes until the peppers are soft. Top with the cheese and air fry for 1 to 2 minutes longer until melted.

Per serving: 445 calories, 33 g protein, 35 g carbohydrates, 19 g fat (8.1 g sat fat), 5 g fibre

Homestyle Meatloaf

Makes 4 servings • Prep time: 15 minutes • Total time: 1 hour

1 small onion, coarsely chopped

1 celery stick, coarsely chopped

2 cloves garlic

450g lean minced beef

1 large egg, lightly beaten

25g panko breadcrumbs

2 tablespoons milk

1 teaspoon salt

½ teaspoon freshly ground black pepper

2 tablespoons tomato ketchup

1 tablespoon brown sugar

Nothing says comfort food like meatloaf, and this one fits the bill with a rich, sweet glaze of ketchup baked into the crust. Because the air fryer circulates hot air while it cooks, your meatloaf will be done a little faster than if you were to bake it in a conventional oven.

1. Preheat the air fryer to 180°C. Lightly coat a 20cm round pan with olive oil and set aside.

2. In a food processor fitted with a metal blade, pulse the onion, celery, and garlic until finely chopped. Transfer the vegetables to a large mixing bowl.

3. Add the beef, egg, breadcrumbs, milk, salt, and pepper. Mix gently until thoroughly combined. Transfer the mixture to the prepared pan and shape into a loaf.

4. In a small bowl, stir together the ketchup and brown sugar. Pour the glaze over the meatloaf and spread evenly with the back of a spoon.

5. Air fry for 45 minutes or until the meatloaf is nicely browned and a meat thermometer inserted into the thickest part reaches 70°C. Remove from the air fryer and leave to rest for about 10 minutes before slicing.

Per serving: 295 calories, 22 g protein, 18 g carbohydrates, 13 g fat (5 g sat fat), 0 g fibre

Breaded Chicken Fingers with Maple-Mustard Dipping Sauce

Makes 4 servings • Prep time: 20 minutes • Total time: 30 minutes + marinating

CHICKEN FINGERS

680g boneless, skinless chicken breasts, cut into fingers

240ml buttermilk

1 teaspoon garlic powder

1 teaspoon salt

½ teaspoon freshly ground black pepper

½ teaspoon dried thyme

45g panko breadcrumbs

2 teaspoons Old Bay or Cajun seasoning

MAPLE-MUSTARD SAUCE

4 tablespoons light golden or maple syrup

4 tablespoons Dijon mustard

Marinating not only infuses flavour but also ensures that a light coating of breadcrumbs will cling to the chicken breast fingers resulting in a far healthier dish. Compared to traditionally deep-fried breaded chicken your air fryer saves you more than 10 grams of fat!

1. To make the chicken: In a large resealable bag, combine the chicken, buttermilk, garlic powder, salt, pepper, and thyme. Seal the bag and massage gently until the chicken is thoroughly coated. Refrigerate for at least 2 hours or overnight.

2. Preheat the air fryer to 200°C.

3. In a large bowl, stir together the breadcrumbs and Old Bay seasoning.

4. Remove the chicken from the marinade, letting most of the marinade drip off before transferring it to the bowl with the breadcrumbs. Toss the chicken gently, pressing lightly to ensure an even coating.

5. Working in batches if necessary, arrange the chicken in a single layer in the air fryer basket and spritz lightly with olive oil. Air fry for 10 to 12 minutes, pausing halfway through the cooking time to turn the chicken, until cooked through.

6. To make the maple-mustard sauce: In a small bowl, stir together the syrup and Dijon until smooth. Serve with the chicken fingers for dipping.

Per serving: 375 calories, 42 g protein, 29 g carbohydrates, 7 g fat (1.7 g sat fat), 1 g fibre

New Classic Fish Fingers

Makes 4 servings • Prep time: 15 minutes • Total time: 30 minutes

FISH FINGERS

680g cod fillets, cut into 2.5cm strips

1 teaspoon salt

½ teaspoon freshly ground black pepper

30g plain flour

2 large eggs

45g panko breadcrumbs

TARTAR SAUCE

100g reduced-fat soured cream

115g reduced-fat mayonnaise

3 tablespoons chopped dill pickle

2 tablespoons capers, drained and chopped

½ teaspoon dried dill

1 tablespoon dill pickle liquid (optional)

If you're feeling nostalgic for a food flashback, try this new version of the classic family favourite. Thanks to the air fryer, you can enjoy great flavour with lightened fat and calories. It will taste far fresher than the fish fingers you buy in the freezer aisle!

1. Preheat the air fryer to 200°C.

2. To make the fish fingers: Season the cod with the salt and pepper and sprinkle with the flour, tossing until the fish is thoroughly coated; set aside.

3. In a shallow bowl, lightly beat the eggs. In a second shallow bowl, place the breadcrumbs.

4. Working with a few pieces at a time, dip the fish into the egg mixture followed by the breadcrumbs. Press lightly to ensure an even coating.

5. Working in batches if necessary, arrange the fish in a single layer in the air fryer basket and spritz lightly with olive oil. Air fry for 12 to 15 minutes, pausing halfway through the cooking time to turn the fish, until the fish flakes easily with a fork. Leave to stand in the basket for a few minutes before serving.

6. To make the tartar sauce: In a small bowl, whisk together the soured cream, mayonnaise, pickle, capers, and dill until thoroughly combined. If you prefer a thinner sauce, stir in the pickle liquid. Serve with the fish fingers.

Per serving: 450 calories, 35 g protein, 32 g carbohydrates, 17 g fat (4.3 g sat fat), 1 g fibre

Spicy Roasted Prawns

Makes 4 servings • Prep time: 5 minutes • Total time: 20 minutes

2 tablespoons olive oil

3 cloves garlic, minced

Juice of 1 lemon

1 teaspoon salt

½ teaspoon freshly ground black pepper

½ teaspoon paprika

¼ teaspoon dried chilli flakes (optional)

680g large uncooked prawns, peeled and deveined

2 tablespoons chopped fresh coriander

Tuck a bag of frozen prawns in the back of your freezer and you'll always be prepared to make this super dish. To thaw prawns quickly (and safely), simply submerge in a bowl of cold water for about 20 minutes. For best results, make sure to pat them dry with paper towels before proceeding with the recipe.

1. Preheat the air fryer to 190°C.

2. In a large bowl, stir together the olive oil, garlic, lemon juice, salt, pepper, paprika, and chilli flakes (if using). Add the prawns and toss until thoroughly coated.

3. Transfer the prawns to the air fryer basket. Air fry for 12 to 15 minutes, pausing halfway through to shake the basket, until the prawns are cooked through.

4. Top with the coriander just before serving.

Per serving: 185 calories, 23 g protein, 3 g carbohydrates, 9 g fat (1.4 g sat fat), 0 g fibre

Better-Than-a-Takeaway Prawns and Broccoli

Makes 4 servings • Prep time: 10 minutes • Total time: 25 minutes

2 tablespoons reduced-salt soy sauce

1 tablespoon sesame oil

2 teaspoons chilli-garlic sauce

3 cloves garlic, minced

1 teaspoon grated fresh ginger

680g large uncooked prawns, peeled and deveined

1 head broccoli, cut into florets

35g sesame seeds

Takeaways can be tempting for convenience, but they often come with a nutritional price. Why not enjoy the flavour of classic Chinese dishes while lightening up the fat and calorie load? Your air fryer makes it simple! And this dish can be ready in the same time it would take you to place an order and wait for delivery or pick it up.

1. Preheat the air fryer to 190°C.

2. In a large bowl, stir together the soy sauce, sesame oil, chilli-garlic sauce, garlic, and ginger. Add the prawns and broccoli and toss until thoroughly coated.

3. Transfer the prawns and broccoli to the air fryer basket. Air fry for 12 to 15 minutes, pausing halfway through the cooking time to shake the basket, until the prawns are cooked through and the broccoli is tender.

4. Top with the sesame seeds just before serving.

Per serving: 245 calories, 28 g protein, 9 g carbohydrates, 11 g fat (1.8 g sat fat), 4 g fibre

Barbecue-Glazed Salmon

Makes 4 servings • Prep time: 10 minutes • Total time: 18 minutes

145g barbecue sauce

2 tablespoons honey

550g salmon fillets

½ teaspoon salt

2 spring onions, thinly sliced

Lining the bottom of your air fryer with a piece of parchment will make cleanup a breeze. However, this is a recipe that requires careful attention. Glaze the salmon lightly at first because the extra sugar in the sauce will make it burn easily if it's in the air fryer too long.

1. Cut a piece of parchment to fit the bottom of the air fryer basket and set aside. Preheat the air fryer to 200°C.

2. In a small bowl, whisk together the barbecue sauce and honey.

3. Sprinkle the fish with the salt and brush lightly with the sauce. Arrange the fish on the parchment, skin-side down, so there is room between the pieces.

4. Air fry for 5 minutes, pausing to baste the fish again with the rest of the sauce. Continue air frying for 3 to 5 minutes longer until the fish is cooked through and flakes easily with a fork.

5. Leave to stand for 5 minutes before serving. Top with the spring onions.

Per serving: 365 calories, 29 g protein, 25 g carbohydrates, 16 g fat (3.2 g sat fat), 0 g fibre

Miso-Glazed Cod

15g unsalted butter, melted

4 tablespoons white miso paste

2 tablespoons honey

1 tablespoon rice wine vinegar

½ teaspoon grated fresh ginger

680g cod

Salt and freshly ground black pepper

1 teaspoon toasted sesame oil

Miso, a classic Japanese condiment, is a fermented soya bean paste that lends a deep flavour to an otherwise mild fish. However, Asian-inspired sides aren't essential. This dish pairs perfectly with a simple salad and boiled new potatoes.

1. Cut a piece of parchment to fit the bottom of the air fryer basket and set aside. Preheat the air fryer to 200°C.

2. In a small bowl, whisk together the butter, miso, honey, vinegar, and ginger until smooth.

3. Season the fish with the salt and pepper, then brush lightly with the oil followed by half of the sauce. Arrange the fish on the parchment so there is room between the pieces.

4. Air fry for 5 minutes, pausing to baste the fish again with the rest of the sauce. Continue air frying for 3 to 5 minutes longer until the fish is cooked through and flakes easily with a fork.

Per serving: 250 calories, 32 g protein, 15 g carbohydrates, 6 g fat (2.4 g sat fat), 1 g fibre

Lemon-Pepper Tilapia

Makes 4 servings • Prep time: 10 minutes • Total time: 18 minutes

680g tilapia or other white fish fillets

2 teaspoons olive oil

2 teaspoons lemon-pepper seasoning, or the grated zest of 1 lemon and salt and freshly ground black pepper

1 teaspoon paprika (optional)

4 lemon slices

Lean proteins can help you feel more satisfied with fewer calories, which makes this fish dish a great choice for a quick weeknight meal. Its naturally mild flavour is anything but boring thanks to a little spice mix.

1. Cut a piece of parchment to fit the bottom of the air fryer basket and set aside. Preheat the air fryer to 200°C.

2. Brush the tilapia lightly with the oil and season both sides with the lemon-pepper seasoning and paprika (if using). Arrange the fish on the parchment so there is room between the pieces.

3. Air fry for 8 minutes until the fish is cooked through and flakes easily with a fork.

4. Serve with the lemon slices.

Per serving: 185 calories, 33 g protein, 0 g carbohydrates, 6 g fat (1.5 g sat fat), 0 g fibre

Fish Tacos with Quick-Pickled Onions and Peppers

Makes 4 servings • Prep time: 20 minutes • Total time: 35 minutes

QUICK-PICKLED ONIONS AND PEPPERS

1 small onion, thinly sliced

1 small jalapeño chilli, seeded and sliced

80ml apple cider vinegar

80ml water

1 teaspoon salt

2 teaspoons sugar

FISH TACOS

680g cod

Salt and freshly ground black pepper

30g plain flour

2 large eggs

45g panko breadcrumbs

55g light mayonnaise

1 tablespoon chipotle hot sauce

8 small flour tortillas

2 tablespoons chopped fresh coriander

2 tablespoons chopped red onion (optional)

This dish has several components, but each is relatively quick to prepare and the results are truly worth it. If you have any leftover pickled onions, cover and refrigerate for up to a week and use in salads and sandwiches.

1. To make the quick-pickled onions and peppers: In a bowl, stir together the onion, jalapeño, vinegar, water, salt, and sugar. Leave to stand while you prepare the tacos.

2. Preheat the air fryer to 200°C.

3. To make the fish tacos: Cut the cod into portions and season with salt and pepper, then sprinkle with flour, tossing until the fish is thoroughly coated; set aside.

4. In a shallow bowl, lightly beat the eggs. In a second shallow bowl, place the breadcrumbs. Working with a few pieces at a time, dip the fish into the egg mixture followed by the breadcrumbs. Press to ensure an even coating.

5. Working in batches if necessary, arrange the fish in a single layer in the air fryer basket and spritz lightly with olive oil. Air fry for 12 to 15 minutes, pausing halfway through the cooking time to turn the fish, until the fish flakes easily with a fork.

6. Meanwhile, in a small bowl, whisk together the mayonnaise and hot sauce. Slather the sauce on the tortillas and top with the fish, pickled onions, coriander, and red onion (if using).

Per serving: 530 calories, 38 g protein, 60 g carbohydrates, 12 g fat (2.2 g sat fat), 2 g fibre

Stacked Black Bean Enchiladas

Makes 4 servings • Prep time: 15 minutes • Total time: 35 minutes

400g can black beans, rinsed and drained

¼ red pepper, finely chopped

3 spring onions, thinly sliced

1 tablespoon chilli powder

280g enchilada sauce, red or green

8 (15cm) corn tortillas

100g reduced-fat soured cream

45g reduced-fat Cheddar cheese, grated

4 tablespoons chopped fresh coriander

Depending on the size of your air fryer, fitting a rectangular dish full of enchiladas can be tricky. Instead, this recipe layers the ingredients into a round baking dish more like a lasagna. Problem solved! As an added bonus, you don't have to preheat the corn tortillas to avoid breaking them as you roll them up.

1. In a large bowl, stir together the beans, pepper, spring onions, and chilli powder until thoroughly combined.

2. Preheat the air fryer to 180°C.

3. Coat the inside of an 18cm round baking dish with olive oil and spread a few spoonfuls of the enchilada sauce evenly in the bottom of the dish. Top with 2 tortillas and spread the following ingredients in even layers: a third of the soured cream, a third of the bean mixture, a quarter of the remaining sauce, and 1 tablespoon of the cheese. Top with 2 tortillas and repeat the layers with the remaining ingredients, ending with 2 tortillas topped with the remaining sauce and cheese.

4. Place the baking dish in the air fryer basket. Air fry for 20 minutes until the cheese is melted and the sauce is bubbling. Leave to rest for 5 minutes.

5. Top with the coriander just before serving.

Per serving: *320 calories, 15 g protein, 46 g carbohydrates, 9 g fat (4.4 g sat fat), 11 g fibre*

Vegetarian Shepherd's Pie

Makes 4 servings • Prep time: 10 minutes • Total time: 40 minutes

2 teaspoons olive oil

1 small onion, chopped

1 small carrot, chopped

Salt and freshly ground black pepper

280g vegetarian mince

80g canned chopped tomatoes

½ teaspoon dried thyme

160g frozen peas

450g mashed potatoes

45g reduced-fat Cheddar cheese, grated

Need an easy comfort casserole that comes together with a few items from your freezer and store cupboard? This vegetarian recipe is a surefire winner for the air fryer.

1. Combine the olive oil, onion, and carrot in an 18cm round baking dish and stir until the vegetables are coated. Season to taste with salt and pepper.

2. Place the baking dish in the air fryer basket and set the air fryer to 180°C. Air fry for 5 minutes until the onion begins to soften.

3. Carefully add the vegetarian mince and air fry for 5 minutes longer until the mince begins to sizzle. Add the tomatoes and thyme and stir until thoroughly combined. Scatter the peas on top of the vegetable mixture and spread the mashed potatoes on top.

4. Air fry for 15 minutes until heated throughout. Scatter the cheese on top and air fry for 5 minutes longer until melted.

Per serving: *330 calories, 25 g protein, 28 g carbohydrates, 10 g fat (3 g sat fat), 5 g fibre*

Cauliflower "Steaks" with Chimichurri Sauce

Makes 2 servings • Prep time: 10 minutes • Total time: 35 minutes

CAULIFLOWER "STEAKS"

1 large head cauliflower

2 teaspoons olive oil

Salt and freshly ground black pepper

CHIMICHURRI SAUCE

2 tablespoons olive oil

2 teaspoons red wine vinegar

2 tablespoons freshly chopped parsley

2 tablespoons freshly chopped coriander

1 clove garlic, minced

½ teaspoon dried oregano

½ teaspoon dried chilli flakes

Salt to taste

Cauliflower is notably low in calories and high in fibre (about 115 calories and 9 grams of fibre per pound)—the reason it plays a starring role in so many weight-loss recipes. However, it can be hard to get each piece perfectly browned, which is why this particular dish is so well suited to preparing in an air fryer.

1. Preheat the air fryer to at 230°C.

2. To make the cauliflower "steaks": Remove any outer leaves from the cauliflower and trim the stem of its cut edges, but leave the stem intact. Place on a cutting board stem-side down. Using a large chef's knife, cut two 1.5cm-thick slices from the centre of the cauliflower (save the remaining cauliflower for another use). Rub the cauliflower with the olive oil and season to taste with salt and pepper.

3. Arrange the cauliflower in the air fryer basket and air fry for 25 to 35 minutes, turning once halfway through, until browned and the stems feel tender when pierced with a knife.

4. To make the chimichurri sauce: In a small bowl, stir together the olive oil, vinegar, parsley, coriander, garlic, oregano, and chilli flakes. Season to taste with salt.

5. Spoon the sauce over the cauliflower steaks just before serving.

Per serving: 215 calories, 4 g protein, 12 g carbohydrates, 18 g fat (2.5 g sat fat), 5 g fibre

Portobello Pizzas

Makes 4 servings • Prep time: 10 minutes • Total time: 20 minutes

160g canned chopped tomatoes

2 cloves garlic, minced

1 teaspoon sugar

½ teaspoon dried oregano

¼ teaspoon dried chilli flakes (optional)

2 tablespoons olive oil

4 large portobello mushrooms, stems removed and gills scraped out

Salt and freshly ground black pepper

175g fresh mozzarella, sliced

200g frozen, thawed spinach, squeezed dry

40g grated Parmesan cheese

1 tablespoon chopped fresh parsley

Craving the taste of a mushroom pizza? Skip the carbs and calories in a traditional crust and enjoy this super-easy healthier version instead.

1. Preheat the air fryer to 200°C.

2. In a small bowl, stir together the tomatoes, garlic, sugar, oregano, and chilli flakes (if using).

3. Rub the olive oil over the portobello mushrooms until thoroughly coated. Sprinkle both sides with salt and pepper. Place top-side down on a clean work surface. Divide the sauce among the mushrooms and top with the mozzarella, spinach, and Parmesan.

4. Working in batches if necessary, transfer the mushrooms to the air fryer basket. Air fry for 10 to 14 minutes until the mushrooms are tender and the cheese has begun to brown. Top with the fresh parsley just before serving.

Per serving: 265 calories, 17 g protein, 11 g carbohydrates, 11 g fat (7.4 g sat fat), 3 g fibre

easy entertaining

Bruschetta with Roasted Tomatoes

Makes 8 servings • Prep time: 10 minutes • Total time: 20 minutes

1 large clove garlic

8 slices French bread (about 225g)

100g baby plum tomatoes, halved

1 tablespoon olive oil

Salt and freshly ground black pepper

50g prepared pesto

55g goat's cheese, crumbled

Zest of 1 lemon

If you dread the idea of giving up bread in order to lose weight, this recipe is for you. Your air fryer makes it easy to control the amount of added fat that is usually loaded onto bruschetta. *Buon appetito!*

1. Preheat the air fryer to 180°C.

2. Slice the garlic in half and rub gently on each piece of bread.

3. Arrange the bread in the air fryer basket and spritz lightly with olive oil. Working in batches if necessary, air fry for 5 minutes until lightly browned. Transfer the bread to a serving plate.

4. Meanwhile, mince the garlic. In a small baking pan, stir together the garlic, tomatoes, and olive oil. Season to taste with salt and pepper. Air fry the tomato mixture for 5 minutes until the tomatoes are soft and beginning to blister.

5. Spread the bread with the pesto. Top with the tomato mixture, cheese, and lemon zest before serving.

Per serving: *160 calories, 6 g protein, 17 g carbohydrates, 8 g fat (2.4 g sat fat), 1 g fibre*

Crispy Brussels Sprouts with Honey-Mustard Dipping Sauce

Makes 4 servings • Prep time: 10 minutes • Total time: 25 minutes

BRUSSELS SPROUTS

450g Brussels sprouts

1 tablespoon olive oil

1 teaspoon dried thyme

Salt and freshly ground black pepper

HONEY-MUSTARD SAUCE

3 tablespoons Dijon mustard

3 tablespoons honey

Crisply cooked Brussels sprouts make a lovely change, especially when served with a dipping sauce. A quick shake in an air fryer basket beats having to turn each piece when baking in a standard oven. If you're concerned about carbs, try dipping them in mustard (without the honey) and you'll save 13 grams of carbs.

1. Preheat the air fryer to 190°C.

2. To make the Brussels sprouts: Trim the Brussels sprouts and halve any that are larger than 2.5cm wide. Transfer to a large bowl, drizzle with the olive oil, sprinkle with the thyme, and season to taste with salt and pepper. Toss until thoroughly coated.

3. Add the Brussels sprouts to the air fryer basket and shake into a single layer. Air fry for 15 minutes, pausing to shake the basket halfway through the cooking time, until browned and beginning to crisp.

4. To make the honey-mustard sauce: In a small bowl, whisk together the Dijon and honey until smooth. Serve with the Brussels sprouts for dipping.

Per serving: 135 calories, 4 g protein, 24 g carbohydrates, 4 g fat (0.6 g sat fat), 5 g fibre

Fried Artichoke Hearts with Aioli

Makes 4 servings • Prep time: 10 minutes • Total time: 17 minutes

FRIED ARTICHOKE HEARTS

2 tablespoons panko breadcrumbs

2 tablespoons grated Parmesan cheese

½ teaspoon dried oregano

½ teaspoon garlic powder

400g can quartered artichokes packed in water, drained

1 tablespoon olive oil

Salt and freshly ground black pepper

AIOLI

55g reduced-fat mayonnaise

2 teaspoons fresh lemon juice

1 to 2 cloves garlic, to taste, minced

Here's a delicious way to start a casual dinner party with friends. Unlike traditional deep-frying, which can often render artichokes a soggy mess, your air fryer guarantees perfect results every time.

1. Preheat the air fryer to 200°C.

2. To make the artichokes: In a small bowl, stir together the breadcrumbs, Parmesan, oregano, and garlic powder until combined.

3. Pat the artichoke hearts dry with a paper towel to remove excess moisture and place in a large bowl. Drizzle with the olive oil and toss to coat. Sprinkle the breadcrumb mixture over the artichokes, season to taste with salt and pepper, and toss again.

4. Arrange the artichokes in the air fryer basket in a single layer. Air fry for 8 minutes, pausing halfway through the cooking time to shake the basket, until the artichokes begin to brown and the edges are crispy.

5. To make the aioli: In a small bowl, whisk together the mayonnaise, lemon juice, and garlic. Serve with the artichoke hearts for dipping.

Per serving: 140 calories, 3 g protein, 10 g carbohydrates, 10 g fat (1.7 g sat fat), 5 g fibre

Spicy Sicilian Chicken Drumsticks

Makes 4 servings • Prep time: 5 minutes • Total time: 30 minutes + marinating time

240ml Italian salad dressing

1 tablespoon minced fresh rosemary, plus additional for garnish (optional)

1 teaspoon dried chilli flakes

2 cloves garlic, minced

8 chicken drumsticks, skin-on

Slim down your drumsticks as well as your time in the kitchen! The secret: create a flavourful marinade with a dressing jump-start and a few fresh add-ins. Prep this dish in the morning and you'll be rewarded with a super-simple and satisfying dinner. If you're counting carbs, serve with a side salad and spiralized courgette ribbons instead of traditional pasta.

1. In a large resealable bag, combine the salad dressing, rosemary, chilli flakes, garlic, and chicken. Massage the bag to ensure the chicken is thoroughly coated; refrigerate for at least 2 hours or overnight.

2. Preheat the air fryer to 180°C.

3. Working in batches if necessary, arrange the drumsticks in the air fryer basket, making sure they do not touch. Discard the marinade. Air fry for 30 to 35 minutes, pausing halfway through the cooking time to turn the chicken, or until the skin is browned and a meat thermometer inserted into the thickest portion reaches 74°C.

4. Serve with additional rosemary sprigs as garnish (if using).

Per serving: 435 calories, 49 g protein, 0.5 g carbohydrates, 25 g fat (6.2 g sat fat), 0 g fibre

Stuffed Chicken Breasts

Makes 4 servings • Prep time: 20 minutes • Total time: 45 minutes

140g fresh spinach

1 shallot, finely chopped

2 tablespoons olive oil, divided

2 tablespoons raisins, finely chopped

1 tablespoon chopped fresh rosemary

Salt and freshly ground black pepper

4 small boneless, skinless chicken breasts (about 680g)

Juice of ½ lemon

Why dirty more pans than necessary? Your air fryer is the perfect tool for cooking fresh spinach for this flavourful dish. Less mess is the key to stress-free entertaining.

1. Preheat the air fryer to 180°C.

2. Place the spinach and shallot in a small dish and drizzle with 1 tablespoon of the olive oil. Place the dish in the air fryer basket and air fry for 5 minutes until the spinach is wilted, pausing halfway through the cooking time to stir the spinach. Transfer the spinach and shallot to a bowl and increase the air fryer temperature to 200°C.

3. Stir the raisins and rosemary into the spinach mixture and season to taste with salt and pepper.

4. Using a sharp knife, cut the chicken breasts, slicing them across and opening them up like a book, but be careful not to cut them all the way through. Sprinkle the chicken with salt and pepper.

5. Spoon equal amounts of the spinach mixture onto each chicken breast, then fold the chicken breast over the top of the stuffing. Secure the chicken with cocktail sticks and drizzle with the remaining 1 tablespoon of oil.

6. Working in batches if necessary, air fry the chicken for 18 to 20 minutes until cooked through and a meat thermometer inserted into the thickest part of the chicken reaches 74°C. Squeeze the lemon juice over the chicken breasts right after taking them out of the air fryer. Leave to rest for 5 minutes and remove the sticks before serving.

Per serving: 285 calories, 40 g protein, 7 g carbohydrates, 11 g fat (2.2 g sat fat), 1 g fibre

Roast Turkey with Cranberry Sauce

Makes 8 servings • Prep time: 10 minutes • Total time: 1 hour

ROAST TURKEY

1 teaspoon salt

1 teaspoon garlic powder

½ teaspoon dried rosemary

½ teaspoon paprika

½ teaspoon freshly ground black pepper

1 boneless, skinless turkey breast (about 1.3kg)

1 tablespoon olive oil

CRANBERRY SAUCE

350g cranberries, fresh or frozen

125ml thawed frozen orange juice concentrate

2 tablespoons maple syrup

60ml water (if needed)

An air fryer can give you so much more flexibility during Christmas, freeing up valuable space in your regular oven for other dishes. But why wait for then when such a delicious meal can fit into your weight loss plans any time of year?

1. To make the roast turkey: In a small bowl, stir together the salt, garlic powder, rosemary, paprika, and pepper.

2. Coat the turkey breast with the olive oil on all sides and rub with the seasoning mixture until thoroughly coated. Place the turkey breast in the air fryer basket and air fry at 180°C for 40 minutes, pausing halfway through to flip the turkey breast, until a meat thermometer inserted into the thickest portion reaches 74°C.

3. To make the cranberry sauce: In a small pan, combine the cranberries, orange juice concentrate, and maple syrup over medium-high heat until the mixture begins to boil. Reduce the heat and simmer, stirring occasionally, for 20 minutes, until most of the cranberries have burst. Add water, 1 tablespoon at a time, if you prefer a thinner sauce.

4. Transfer the turkey to a cutting board and allow to rest 15 minutes before slicing and serving with the sauce.

TIP: Given the longer roasting time, there's no need to preheat your air fryer with this dish.

Per serving: 260 calories, 39 g protein, 14 g carbohydrates, 4 g fat (1 g sat fat), 2 g fibre

Pistachio-Crusted Chicken with Pomegranate Glaze

Makes 4 servings • Prep time: 10 minutes • Total time: 20 minutes

2 boneless, skinless chicken breasts (about 680g)

Salt and freshly ground black pepper

55g reduced-fat mayonnaise

60g shelled pistachios, chopped

140g baby rocket

2 tablespoons pomegranate or balsamic glaze, for garnish

Some research suggests that eating nuts regularly may play an important role in helping you lose weight because they are loaded with monounsaturated fats. However, the real reason to enjoy them is because they are so delicious! Instead of using eggs and flour to make an air fryer feast, this dish relies on reduced-calorie mayonnaise to help the nuts form a crunchy coating.

1. Cut a piece of parchment paper to fit the bottom of the air fryer basket. Preheat the air fryer to 200°C.

2. Starting on the thicker side, use a long, sharp knife to slice each chicken breast horizontally, cutting until you have reached the other side, to make 4 cutlets. Season with salt and pepper. Spread a thin layer of mayonnaise on both sides of the cutlets.

3. Place the pistachios in a shallow dish and dredge the chicken in the nuts, pressing gently to form an even coating. Arrange the cutlets on the parchment paper in the air fryer basket so they're not touching. Air fry for 8 to 10 minutes until browned and cooked through.

4. Leave to rest for 5 minutes before serving on a bed of rocket drizzled with the glaze for garnish.

Per serving: *360 calories, 43 g protein, 8 g carbohydrates, 18 g fat (3 g sat fat), 2 g fibre*

Hawaiian Pork Chops with Pineapple

Makes 4 servings • Prep time: 10 minutes • Total time: 20 minutes + marinating time

3 tablespoons Worcestershire sauce

1 tablespoon brown sugar

1 tablespoon grated fresh ginger

½ teaspoon dried chilli flakes (optional)

4 large pork chops (about 680g)

4 slices fresh pineapple, each about 1cm thick

2 spring onions, thinly sliced

Pork and pineapple are the perfect combination, especially when you use an air fryer—the pineapple will caramelize as it cooks on top of the meat. Serve on a bed of brown rice or alongside a colourful coleslaw salad.

1. In a shallow dish, stir together the Worcestershire sauce, brown sugar, ginger, and chilli flakes (if using) until smooth. Add the pork, turning to coat, and marinate at room temperature for 30 minutes, turning once.

2. Preheat the air fryer to 200°C.

3. Arrange the pork in the air fryer basket so the pieces do not touch and spritz lightly with olive oil. Air fry for 10 minutes, pausing halfway through the cooking time to turn the chops and set a pineapple ring on top of each chop, until browned and a meat thermometer inserted into the thickest portion reaches 63°C.

4. Leave to rest for 5 minutes before serving topped with the spring onions.

Per serving: *325 calories, 38 g protein, 13 g carbohydrates, 13 g fat (4.6 g sat fat), 1 g fibre*

Roast Beef
with Horseradish Cream

Makes 6 servings • Prep time: 10 minutes • Total time: 45 minutes

ROAST BEEF

900g beef topside or top rump

1 tablespoon salt

2 teaspoons garlic powder

1 teaspoon freshly ground black pepper

1 teaspoon dried thyme

HORSERADISH CREAM

3 tablespoons semi-skimmed milk

3 tablespoons single cream

70g reduced-fat soured cream

5 tablespoons creamed horseradish

2 teaspoons fresh lemon juice

Salt and freshly ground black pepper

A classic beef roast is an easy way to impress guests without derailing your weight loss goals. Serve with a simple salad or the Crispy Brussels Sprouts on page 100.

1. Preheat the air fryer to 200°C.

2. To make the roast beef: Season the beef with the salt, garlic powder, pepper, and thyme. Place the beef fat-side down in the air fryer basket and lightly spritz with olive oil. Air fry for 35 to 45 minutes, pausing halfway through the cooking time to turn the beef, until a meat thermometer inserted into the thickest part indicates the desired doneness, 52°C (rare) to 65°C (medium). Leave the beef to rest for 10 minutes before slicing.

3. To make the horseradish cream: In a small bowl, whisk together the milk, cream, soured cream, horseradish, and lemon juice until thoroughly combined. Season to taste with salt and pepper. Serve alongside the beef.

Per serving: 235 calories, 35 g protein, 4 g carbohydrates, 8 g fat (3.3 g sat fat), 0 g fibre

Steak Tips with Mushrooms

Makes 4 servings • Prep time: 10 minutes • Total time: 20 minutes + marinating time

680g sirloin, trimmed and cut into 2.5cm pieces

225g chestnut mushrooms, halved

60ml Worcestershire sauce

1 tablespoon Dijon mustard

1 tablespoon olive oil

1 teaspoon paprika

1 teaspoon dried chilli flakes

¼ red onion, thinly sliced

2 tablespoons chopped fresh parsley (optional)

Cooking steak in an air fryer can be tricky because it's easy to accidentally overcook the meat. This recipe gives you a little more wiggle room because the marinade helps keep the steak tender and juicy. For a true steakhouse experience, serve with baked potatoes and a salad of lettuce wedges with a light dressing.

1. Place the beef and mushrooms in a large resealable bag. In a small bowl, whisk together the Worcestershire, mustard, olive oil, paprika, and chilli flakes. Add the onion and stir to combine. Pour the marinade into the bag and massage gently to ensure the beef and mushrooms are evenly coated. Seal the bag and refrigerate for at least 4 hours, preferably overnight. Remove from the refrigerator 30 minutes before cooking.

2. Preheat the air fryer to 200°C.

3. Drain and discard the marinade. Arrange the steak and mushrooms in the air fryer basket. Air fry for 10 minutes, pausing halfway through the baking time to shake the basket, until the mushrooms are browned and the steak tips are cooked to the desired doneness when tested with a meat thermometer, 52°C (rare) to 65°C (medium). Transfer to a serving plate and top with the parsley (if using).

Per serving: 330 calories, 41 g protein, 2 g carbohydrates, 17 g fat (6.2 g sat fat), 0 g fibre

Swordfish Steaks with Cucumber Salsa

Makes 2 servings • Prep time: 20 minutes • Total time: 30 minutes

SWORDFISH

2 teaspoons honey

2 teaspoons reduced-salt soy sauce

2 swordfish steaks (about 350g)

CUCUMBER SALSA

1 cucumber, peeled, seeded, and chopped

½ jalapeño chilli seeded and finely chopped

1 spring onion, thinly sliced

Juice of ½ lime

2 tablespoons chopped fresh mint or coriander

Salt and freshly ground black pepper

This easy honey-soy marinade works well with most fish, but the cucumber salsa is a perfect complement to the rich, oily texture of swordfish. You can use either mint or coriander in the salsa, whichever you prefer.

1. To make the swordfish: In a shallow dish, stir together the honey and soy sauce until smooth. Add the swordfish, turning to coat, and marinate at room temperature for 15 minutes, turning once. Preheat the air fryer to 200°C while the fish marinates.

2. To make the cucumber salsa: In a small bowl, stir together the cucumber, jalapeño, spring onion, lime juice, and mint or coriander. Season to taste with salt and pepper.

3. Place the fish in the air fryer basket and spritz with olive oil. Air fry for 10 minutes, pausing halfway through the cooking time to flip the fish, until cooked through and a fork slips easily through the fish.

4. Serve the swordfish topped with the salsa.

TIP: To minimize mercury exposure, most health experts recommend limiting your intake of large fish like swordfish (pregnant women should avoid it altogether), but for special occasions swordfish is a fitting treat.

Per serving: 265 calories, 31 g protein, 10 g carbohydrates, 10 g fat (2.5 g sat fat), 1 g fibre

Crab Cakes with Roasted Corn-Pepper Relish

Makes 4 servings • Prep time: 20 minutes • Total time: 35 minutes

ROASTED CORN-PEPPER RELISH

200g can sweetcorn, drained

¼ red pepper, seeded and finely chopped

1 teaspoon sugar

1 tablespoon rice wine vinegar

1 teaspoon unsalted butter

CRAB CAKES

225g white crab meat

2 large eggs, beaten

45g panko breadcrumbs

5 tablespoons reduced-fat mayonnaise

1 tablespoon Dijon mustard

1 teaspoon Old Bay or Cajun seasoning

½ teaspoon salt

1 tablespoon chipotle hot sauce

Zest of 1 lemon

Chopped fresh parsley, for garnish

These crab cakes are sure to draw rave reviews whether you serve them as a main dish or an appetizer. For appetizer-size portions, shape the crab mixture into smaller patties and reduce the time in the air fryer to 5 to 7 minutes.

1. Preheat the air fryer to 180°C.

2. To make the relish: In a small baking pan, combine the sweetcorn, pepper, and sugar. Air fry for 5 minutes until the pepper is softened. Remove from the air fryer and stir in the vinegar and butter. Set aside and continue to preheat the air fryer.

3. Meanwhile, to make the crab cakes: In a large bowl, combine the crab meat, eggs, half the breadcrumbs, 3 tablespoons of the mayonnaise, the Dijon, Old Bay seasoning, and salt.

4. Use an ice cream scoop to form the crab mixture patties. Place the patties on a piece of parchment paper cut to fit the dimensions of your air fryer basket, then press lightly with the bottom of the scoop to flatten the patties into a circle about 1cm thick. Press the remaining breadcrumbs on top and spritz lightly with olive oil. Air fry for 10 minutes until lightly browned.

5. In a small bowl, combine the remaining 2 tablespoons of mayonnaise and the chipotle sauce, stirring until smooth.

6. Serve the crab cakes over the corn-pepper relish and top with the chipotle sauce, lemon zest, and parsley.

Per serving: 335 calories, 19 g protein, 34 g carbohydrates, 12 g fat (2.6 g sat fat), 1 g fibre

sweet treats

Glazed Doughnuts

Makes 4 doughnuts • Prep time: 10 minutes • Total time: 17 minutes

DOUGHNUTS

130g plain flour

1½ teaspoons baking powder

½ teaspoon salt

160g vanilla nonfat Greek yogurt

GLAZE

75g icing sugar

15g unsalted butter, melted

½ teaspoon vanilla extract

1½ teaspoons hot water

1 or 2 drops food colouring (optional)

Edible cake decorations (optional)

Decadent doughnuts don't need to take all day or consume all your daily calories! Traditional yeast doughnuts work well in an air fryer, but they require extra time to let the dough rise. A ready-to-go package of biscuit dough makes for speedier prep, but this easy recipe offers an even better way to make your doughnuts lower in fat and just as delicious.

1. To make the doughnuts: In a large bowl, stir together the flour, baking powder, and salt. Add the yogurt and mix until shaggy, then knead in the bowl until the dough holds together in a ball.

2. Divide the dough into 4 equal pieces. On a lightly floured work surface, roll each piece into a ball and pat into a disk about 1cm thick. Poke your finger through the centre of each disk to form into a doughnut shape.

3. Place the doughnuts in the air fryer with space between them. Spray the doughnuts lightly with cooking spray. Air fry for 7 minutes at 350°F, flipping halfway through, until golden brown.

4. To make the glaze: In a small bowl, stir together the icing sugar, butter, vanilla, and water until smooth. Stir in the food colouring (if using).

5. When the doughnuts are cool enough to handle, dip the tops into the glaze and sprinkle on decorations (if using). Serve warm.

Per serving: 240 calories, 8 g protein, 44 g carbohydrates, 3.5 g fat (2 g sat fat), 1 g fibre

Cinnamon Apple Chips

Makes 4 servings • Prep time: 5 minutes • Cook time: 20–25 minutes

30g unsalted butter, melted

1 tablespoon brown sugar

½ teaspoon ground cinnamon

Pinch of salt

2 large apples, such as Gala, cored

Delicious and true: chips can be part of your slim lifestyle! Your air fryer makes a crunchy and sweet treat out of classic apples. It's an easy way to mix up your snack routine while reaching your fruit and vegetable goals.

1. In a large bowl, stir together the butter, brown sugar, cinnamon, and salt.

2. Slice the apples into thin disks using a mandoline slicer, or slice as thinly as possible using a knife.

3. Gently toss the apple slices with the butter mixture until thoroughly coated.

4. Place the apple slices in the air fryer basket, making sure they don't overlap. Set to 180°C and air fry in batches until crispy, about 20 to 25 minutes, pausing once or twice during the cooking time to shake the basket and flip the chips.

5. The chips will become crispier as they cool. Store in a covered container at room temperature.

Per serving: 140 calories, 0 g protein, 21 g carbohydrates, 6 g fat (4 g sat fat), 2.5 g fibre

Caramel-Pecan Popcorn

Makes 4 servings • Prep time: 10 minutes • Total time: 1 hour

25g air-popped popcorn

30g pecans, chopped

50g dark brown sugar

2 tablespoons golden syrup

15g unsalted butter

¼ teaspoon vanilla extract

⅛ teaspoon bicarbonate of soda

⅛ teaspoon salt

It's easy to get swept away by the high heat of an air fryer. But you can produce magical results at a lower temperature, too. Caramel popcorn is a gourmet treat at a fraction of the store-bought cost (and calories).

1. Place the popcorn and nuts in a large bowl and set aside. Generously spritz the air fryer basket with a neutral-flavoured oil, such as avocado. Line a baking sheet with parchment paper.

2. In a small, heavy-bottomed saucepan over medium heat, combine the brown sugar, syrup, and butter and bring to a boil. Cook 2 to 3 minutes, stirring three or four times to scrape down the sides of the pan and keep the mixture from bubbling up. If you have a pastry brush, dip it in cool water and use it to brush down the sides of the pan. Remove from the heat; stir in the vanilla, baking soda, and salt.

3. Preheat the air fryer to 120°C.

4. Carefully pour the sugar mixture over the popcorn in a steady stream, stirring with a silicone spatula until thoroughly coated.

5. Transfer the popcorn mixture to the air fryer basket. Air fry for 45 minutes, stirring every 15 minutes with a silicone spatula, until the mixture begins to look dry.

6. Spread the popcorn on the prepared baking sheet, breaking up any large clumps. The popcorn will harden as it cools. Store in an airtight container for up to 1 week.

Per serving: 180 calories, 1 g protein, 28 g carbohydrates, 8 g fat (2.3 g sat fat), 2 g fibre

Almond Cookies

Makes 18 cookies • Prep time: 10 minutes • Total time: 35 minutes

260g almonds

200g sugar

2 large egg whites

½ teaspoon almond extract

Bite into the crunchy exterior of these delicious cookies and you'll find a sweet chewy interior. Use blanched (skinless) almonds if you prefer lighter coloured cookies, but if you're in a pinch regular almonds will taste just as wonderful.

1. Cut a piece of parchment to fit the air fryer basket, and preheat the air fryer to 150°C.

2. In a food processor, grind the almonds into a fine meal. Add the sugar and whirl for another 15 seconds. Add the egg whites and almond extract and continue to whirl for another 15 seconds until a smooth dough forms around the blade.

3. Using a teaspoon, shape the dough into 18 equal portions. Working in batches, arrange the cookies in the air fryer so they are at least 4cm apart. Air fry for 25 to 30 minutes, pausing halfway through the baking time to flatten the cookies slightly with the back of a spoon, until golden.

TIP: Just four ingredients create amazing, gluten-free cookies!

Per cookie: 135 calories, 4 g protein, 15 g carbohydrates, 8 g fat (0.6 g sat fat), 2 g fibre

Peanut Butter Chocolate Chip Cookies

Makes 16 cookies • Prep time: 5 minutes • Total time: 10 minutes

225g creamy peanut butter

200g brown sugar

1 large egg

½ teaspoon vanilla extract

80g plain mini chocolate chips

Five-ingredient cookies that taste amazingly rich? You bet! Your air fryer makes it easy to whip up small batches of homemade treats, giving you the power to satisfy your cravings—without having dozens of extra cookies lingering around the kitchen to tempt you further. If you're serious about watching carbs, this recipe works well with sugar replacements, such as Pure Via (erythritol).

1. Preheat the air fryer to 180°C. Lightly spritz the air fryer basket with a neutral-flavoured oil, such as avocado.

2. In a large bowl, combine the peanut butter, brown sugar, egg, and vanilla. Using a mixer, beat until thoroughly combined. Stir in the chocolate chips and divide the dough into 16 equal pieces.

3. Shape the dough into balls and flatten slightly with the back of a spoon.

4. Working in batches if necessary, arrange the cookies in the air fryer basket so they are not touching. Air fry for 5 minutes until browned. Leave to cool in the basket for 5 minutes before carefully transferring to a rack to finish cooling.

Per cookie: *180 calories, 4 g protein, 21 g carbohydrates, 10 g fat (2.7 g sat fat), 1 g fibre*

Chocolate Lava Cake for Two

Makes 2 servings • Prep time: 10 minutes • Total time: 20 minutes

40g plain chocolate chips

30g unsalted butter

35g icing sugar

1 large egg

¼ teaspoon vanilla extract

Pinch of salt

1 tablespoon plain flour

60g fresh raspberries

Need a dessert for a romantic night? This fancy lava cake is designed to share from the same plate. The key to success is not overbaking the cake so that the rich chocolate centre oozes out when you cut into it with your fork. It's definitely one to save for special occasions, but the splurge is worth it.

1. Preheat the air fryer to 190°C. Lightly spritz a 240ml ramekin with a neutral-flavoured oil, such as avocado.

2. In a large microwave-safe bowl, combine the chocolate chips and butter. Microwave on high for 1 minute until the butter is melted and the chips are beginning to melt. Whisk until smooth.

3. Add the icing sugar, egg, vanilla, and salt and whisk until smooth. Add the flour and stir just until the flour is incorporated. Transfer the chocolate mixture to the prepared ramekin.

4. Place the ramekin in the air fryer basket. Air fry for 8 to 10 minutes until the top appears slightly puffed and dry. Leave to rest for about 1 minute.

5. Use a butter knife to loosen the sides and turn over onto a plate. Serve decorated with the raspberries.

Per serving: 335 calories, 5 g protein, 36 g carbohydrates, 21 g fat (12 g sat fat), 3 g fibre

Cheesecake Bites

Makes 15 servings • Prep time: 10 minutes • Total time: 20 minutes + chilling time

270g package filo pastry, thawed if frozen

115g package Neufchâtel or Brie

50g sugar

1 tablespoon fresh lemon zest

125ml fat-free nondairy whipped topping

15 fresh raspberries

Heading to a party? Make a batch of these dainty cheesecake bites to take along and you're guaranteed to have something delicious for you to enjoy without blowing your calorie budget.

1. Preheat the air fryer to 180°C.

2. Lightly oil each filo sheet and stack together. Cut into 15 squares. Put a stacked square into a silicon muffin cup. Repeat to fill another 4 muffin cups. Place the muffin cups in the air fryer leaving space between them. Air fry for 5 to 7 minutes until golden. Carefully transfer the filo cases to a baking sheet and repeat with the remaining filo squares to make 15 cups in total, working in batches. Leave to cool completely before filling.

3. Meanwhile, using a mixer fitted with a paddle attachment, beat the Neufchâtel, sugar, and lemon zest until smooth. Use a silicone spatula to carefully fold the whipped topping into the cheese mixture until thoroughly combined.

4. Fill each shell with about a scant tablespoon of the cheese mixture and top with a raspberry. Cover and refrigerate for 2 hours before serving.

Per serving: 50 calories, 1 g protein, 7 g carbohydrates, 2 g fat (1 g sat fat), 0 g fibre

Strawberry Shortcake

Makes 4 servings • Prep time: 20 minutes • Total time: 32 minutes

280g strawberries, sliced

1 tablespoon honey

100g plain flour, plus more for dusting

2 tablespoons sugar

¾ teaspoon baking powder

¼ teaspoon salt

30g unsalted butter

80ml low-fat buttermilk

1 large egg, lightly beaten

½ teaspoon vanilla extract

240ml fat-free nondairy whipped topping

Nothing says summer like strawberry shortcake! It's the perfect way to end lunch and your air fryer is guaranteed to make it so very easy. Letting the strawberries sit in the honey for a bit will draw out the sweetest juices.

1. In a large bowl, combine the strawberries and honey. Stir until the strawberries are thoroughly coated. Set aside.

2. Preheat the air fryer to 200°C.

3. In another large bowl, stir together the flour, sugar, baking powder, and salt. Add the butter and work it into the flour mixture with your fingers until it resembles breadcrumbs.

4. In a small bowl, whisk together the buttermilk, egg, and vanilla. Add to the flour mixture and stir until a dough forms.

5. Turn the dough out onto a lightly floured work surface and divide into 4 pieces. Shape each piece into a biscuit about 1cm thick.

6. Arrange the biscuits in the air fryer basket so they are not touching. Air fry for 12 to 15 minutes until golden. When the biscuits are cool enough to handle, split in half.

7. Sandwich the strawberries and topping between the halved biscuits, then top with more strawberry mixture and topping.

Per serving: 290 calories, 7 g protein, 48 g carbohydrates, 9 g fat (4.9 g sat fat), 4 g fibre

Cherry Turnovers

Makes 8 servings • Prep time: 20 minutes • Total time: 30 minutes

2 x 320g packs ready-rolled puff pastry, thawed if frozen

145g all-fruit cherry preserve

1 large egg, lightly beaten

2 tablespoons sugar

Traditional pies are tricky to bake in an air fryer because, unlike a conventional oven, the heating element is positioned in the top of the unit so the bottom crust has little opportunity to become crisp. These tender, flaky turnovers, however, cook quickly and benefit from the hot air that circulates all around them.

1. Preheat the air fryer to 180°C.

2. Unroll the pastry on a lightly floured surface. Cut each sheet into 4 squares.

3. Place a tablespoon of preserve in the centre of each square. Working one at a time, fold one corner of the dough over and press against the opposite corner to form a triangle. Use a fork to crimp the edges. Use the tip of a knife to cut a small hole in the top so steam can escape. Brush the pies with the egg and sprinkle with the sugar.

4. In batches if necessary, arrange the pies in the air fryer basket so they are not touching. Air fry for 8 to 10 minutes until golden. Serve warm or at room temperature.

Per serving: *300 calories, 3 g protein, 30 g carbohydrates, 15 g fat (5.7 g sat fat), 1 g fibre*

Baked Apples

Makes 4 servings • Prep time: 10 minutes • Total time: 25 minutes

2 red dessert apples

30g pecans, chopped

2 tablespoons brown sugar

15g unsalted butter, softened

1 tablespoon sultanas

Pinch of ground cinnamon

Pinch of salt

Most air fryer baskets have a drip pan beneath them. Adding a little water to the basket helps create steam that will transform these apples into a delicious dessert without becoming soggy. If you're more of a pear fan, this recipe works just as well with pears, too.

1. Preheat the air fryer to 180°C.

2. Cut the apples in half and use a melon baller to remove the core and some of the flesh (leave the skin on).

3. In a small bowl, stir together the pecans, brown sugar, butter, sultanas, cinnamon, and salt. Fill the apple cavities with the nut mixture, pressing gently to ensure the filling holds its shape.

4. Pour 125ml water into the bottom of the air fryer basket to fill the drip pan. Arrange the apples in the air fryer basket. Air fry for 15 minutes until the apples are soft and the tops are beginning to brown.

Per serving: 165 calories, 1 g protein, 24 g carbohydrates, 8 g fat (2.2 g sat fat), 4 g fibre

Honey-Roasted Bananas

Makes 2 servings • Prep time: 5 minutes • Total time: 10 minutes

2 large bananas, peeled

1 tablespoon honey

Pinch of ground cinnamon

Craving something sweet? Your air fryer is the perfect appliance for transforming that plain-looking bunch of bananas on your worktop into an amazing dessert. Serve with a small scoop of sugar-free vanilla ice cream for an extra treat.

1. Preheat the air fryer to 190°C. Cut a piece of parchment to fit the air fryer basket.

2. Slice the bananas in half lengthwise and arrange cut-side down on the parchment, leaving space in between so they are not touching. Drizzle with the honey and sprinkle with a pinch of cinnamon. Use your finger to spread the honey if necessary.

3. Air fry for 5 minutes until the bananas are beginning to brown.

Per serving: 155 calories, 2 g protein, 40 g carbohydrates, 0 g fat (0 g sat fat), 4 g fibre

Almond-Stuffed Peaches

Makes 4 servings • Prep time: 15 minutes • Total time: 45 minutes

2 large peaches

120g almonds, finely chopped

1 large egg white

50g brown sugar

¼ teaspoon almond extract

Pinch of ground cinnamon

Peaches are a tricky fruit because they continue to ripen after being picked. To enjoy peaches at the peak of ripeness, take a sniff. They should have a rich, strong scent. Other signs to look for are a deeper, golden yellow just around the stem and a slight yield when pressed gently with your thumb.

1. Preheat the air fryer to 180°C.

2. Cut the peaches in half and remove the pits (do not peel). Arrange cut-side up in a shallow baking dish that fits your air fryer.

3. In a small bowl, stir together the almonds, egg white, brown sugar, almond extract, and cinnamon until thoroughly combined.

4. Fill the cavities of each peach half with the almond mixture, pressing gently to ensure it holds its shape. Spritz lightly with a neutral-flavoured cooking oil, such as avocado oil. Cover with foil.

5. Air fry for 25 minutes until the peaches are tender. Remove the foil and continue air frying for another 5 minutes until the tops are browned.

Per serving: 205 calories, 6 g protein, 28 g carbohydrates, 9 g fat (0.7 g sat fat), 4 g fibre

Blueberry Crisp

Makes 6 servings • Prep time: 10 minutes • Total time: 50 minutes

100g porridge oats

30g plain flour

50g brown sugar

¼ teaspoon salt

45g unsalted butter, melted

500g blueberries

50g granulated sugar

1 tablespoon cornflour

1 tablespoon fresh lemon juice

¼ teaspoon grated nutmeg

6 small scoops no-sugar vanilla ice cream (optional)

When summer blueberry season hits, this is the dessert you'll want to put at the top of your list. It's so easy to assemble, and with the convenience of an air fryer you'll hardly notice that you've got something baking until the aroma hits you.

1. Preheat the air fryer to 180°C. Lightly coat a 1.7 litre baking dish that fits in your air fryer with cooking spray. Set aside.

2. In a large bowl, stir together the oats, flour, brown sugar, and salt until thoroughly combined. Stir in the butter and mix with a fork until clumps begin to form. Set aside.

3. Place the blueberries in the prepared baking dish. Sprinkle with the granulated sugar, cornflour, lemon juice, and nutmeg. Stir gently until the blueberries are coated. Spread into an even layer and top with the oat mixture.

4. Air fry for 40 minutes until the top is golden and the berries are bubbling. Leave to cool slightly before serving topped with ice cream (if using).

Per serving: 250 calories, 3 g protein, 46 g carbohydrates, 7 g fat (3.8 g sat fat), 4 g fibre

index